Dreaming Money

A Process-Oriented Aproach to Unifying the Worlds of Money, Psychology, and Spirituality

Gary Reiss, LCSW, PhD

Certified Trainer in Process-Oriented Psychology

Copyright ©2013 by Gary Reiss

All rights reserved. No part of this book, in part or in whole, may be reproduced, transmitted, or utilized, in any form or by any means, electronic or mechanical, including photocopying, recording, or by any information storage and retrieval system, without permission in writing from the publisher, except for brief quotations in critical articles, books and reviews.

Cover illustration by Qahira Lynn
Cover and book design by Christine Beneda, Beneda Design

International Standard Book Number: 978-1481907750

First Edition 2013

Address all inquiries to:
Gary Reiss
412 W. 17th
Eugene, OR 97401

Email:greiss@igc.org
Website:http://www.garyreiss.com

ACKNOWLEDGEMENTS

I want to acknowledge my father, Barney Reiss, provided ongoing training and dialogue about the role of money in life. I also want to thank Dr. Arny and Dr. Amy Mindell for developing Process-Oriented Psychology that is the core of the theory of Dreaming Money, and especially Arny Mindell for helping me move through various developmental phases in my personal development and relationship to money.

In terms of the production of this book, I want to thank Qahira Lynn for the cover artwork; Christine Beneda for the layout work, and Lynz Om for editing.

TABLE OF CONTENTS

Introduction 7

Section I—Spiritual Traditions and Money

Chapter 1: Wisdom from the East 21

Chapter 2: Kaballah and Money 37

Section II—Process-Oriented Psychology, Money, and My Story

Chapter 3: Process-oriented Psychology 53
and Dreaming Money

Chapter 4: My Story, Your Story, and Money 109

Chapter 5: Family Issues and Money 135

Section III—Getting of the Wheel of Money

Chapter 6: Addicted to Money 151

Chapter 7: Beyond Addiction, ... 155
Getting off the Wheel

Chapter 8: Sage Emery's Abundance Approach 165

Chapter 9: From Heaven to Earth, ... 183
a 2000's Approach to Self Sufficiency

Chapter 10: Taoist approaches to Money 197

Chapter 11: Conclusion 201

Bibliography 207

Index 209

INTRODUCTION

Spirituality and Money have been portrayed as ancient enemies engaged in eternal conflict. Chose one or the other we are often told; either walk a spiritual or a material path. A life seeking money without spirit is a trap, parallel to that of focusing on our spiritual life and ignoring our financial. Even through lighthearted entertainment, this portrayal of an inherent separation between the two is fed to us. Sitting in the movie theatre, do you remember watching a movie where the robber points his gun to the victim and says, "Your money or your life?" Yet, money and living and spirituality are crucially connected.

For many, the way life presents itself provides the option of either focusing on making money, or living in a way that may feel more meaningful, such as nourishing one's relationships, family, body, and spirituality. In *Dreaming Money*, we look at the central question—is there a way to make money in a less painful and more beneficial approach? Money is enormously addictive and the drive for acquiring money can be overwhelmingly consuming, surpassing the survival level and our basic needs. The trick is to learn to stay conscious in the world of money; a world that is so full of distinctive, potential pitfalls.

I recently read an article in the local newspaper declaring that it is no longer possible to retire on one million dollars; consequently, you must keep working those *eighty* hour weeks until you earn a few million more. How do we know what is real, when we are constantly fed advertising from the media telling us that we must keep making money so we can continue to buy and acquire more things? Money appears so materialistic. What does money have to do with the world of dreams? Does money have anything to do with spirit, does it come from spirit, and is it meant to serve something spiritual, or is it merely material? How can I manifest money for what I need in life, not just through hard work, but through something that is more magical and mystical? These are some of the basic questions I address in this book. I draw from ancient traditions including Judaism, Taoism, Hinduism, Buddhism, and Christianity to address these questions.

I also utilize a psychological approach, Process-oriented Psychology, to study the dreaming aspect to money. In addition I bring in examples from my own life and family history, along with my clients' work from my private therapy practice, to explicate how these principles of various traditions participate in our day-to-day lives. I take the central position that it is vital to our quality of life and experiences to live inspired by our whole selves, including our consensus reality skills of making and managing money. Consensus reality skills refers to our ability to deal with everyday reality in a way that society agrees or consents to as what is real and necessary.

The realm of money is so saturated with tricky turns, much through the attempts by corporations and the media to impart their values into us as to what is "real," and what "we need." Therefore it is essential that we have access to our deepest dreaming nature in order to stay awake in the midst of this confusion. We need for our dreams to stay awake in our lives. By our dreaming nature, I mean our night dreams, as well as our dreamlike waking experiences.

Since I began this book, times have changed. The United States has been in and is just coming out of a major recession.

The European Union has had an enormous financial crisis that has specifically focused on Greece, Portugal, Ireland, and Spain, but has impacted the whole world. In a time when outer financial realities become even more stressful and desperate, we need a way to relate to money that not only takes all of this into reality, but extends much deeper into its relationship with that which moves and fills us with the vitality of life.

We need a connection to our deepest selves that can guide us from the inside in how to work with money. Our deepest essence cries out for our dreams to guide us and for the wisdom of the universe to empower us through what can be scary, treacherous waters.

Someday it is my hope that people will have as easy an access to their dreaming natures around money as they do balancing their checkbook; that they would have a sense of moving fluidly between the more dreamlike aspects of money and the consensus reality tasks of paying their bills. Without the channel into my dreaming nature, I would certainly have become financially and spiritually broke. With my dreaming nature intact, my financial security is working out comfortably, and my relationship to money has become more and more balanced.

Having myself bounced between the poles of disregarding money and not possessing it, to being driven and dominated by money to the point of almost an addiction, I now experience an increasing balance between money and freedom, and this is the path I want to share with you. *Dreaming Money* provides you with the tools that helped free me from the painful cycle of money difficulties, from my own private version of being trapped on the wheel of fate, unable to see or even fathom a way to get off.

When I work with people on their earliest and most positive encounters with money, they often have incredibly emotional experiences, and even spiritual awakenings. In a recent seminar that I facilitated, a woman working on her positive childhood experiences with money suddenly felt her whole being filled with light and she was literally in ecstasy. Coming down from this high, she felt that she had the renewed confidence she needed to turn her financial life around.

My hope is that in my books and through my working with people, I can help make life, especially the daily mundane parts of life—such as money—less scary, less painful, and more and more full of vitality, levity, and fun. This is what motivates me to maintain the focus to continue to work with family life, sexuality, and money, in order to help elevate the mundane to the sacred, by healing this division that we feel between them.

Finally, in this book, I explore social issues that affect money, including racism, classism, sexism, and how we can build this into an awareness of our money consciousness. Otherwise, any discussion of finances marginalizes the incredible diversity of financial well-being that exits on the planet, and this book would consequently only have been written for the middle and upper class; solely reaching those who are well off. Part of our illusion system around money can only exist if we ignore the rest of the world.

For example, one of my friends recently complained about how tight things are for him, and his income exceeds $60,000 a month, in addition to his partner's income. You can only complain about such things if you can ignore that so much of the world lives on less than $60 a month. If the principles that I am writing about on the topic of finances are basic principles, similar to how nature operates, then these standards should be applicable worldwide, and be useful for the global money set up.

I grew up in a wealthy suburb I thought was incredibly materialistic for my pallet, in a family that was also more concerned with money than I felt comfortable with. Even though my family was not wealthy when I was growing up, I was aware of the wealth that surrounded me at school and in my neighborhood in the suburbs. Being a child of the hippy generation, I grew up with a huge split in my consciousness around money. I needed it, suffered from not having it, and yet felt that somehow my being poor protected me from something negative and destructive; the same way in which my parents felt having money kept them safe. Yet, being so against money meant that I was constantly plagued by not having it, and I was endlessly worrying about bills and dentists and car repairs and whatever else it takes to survive and achieve success in modern life.

One day I awoke to a fresh insight. I was listening to my brother, sister, brother-in-law, and father talk about their investments, and the amount of money they had made in the stock market. I noticed my usual feeling of superiority and disgust evolve with the topic of investments, and then suddenly I had a genuine "aha" experience. I thought to myself, "Who planned this game board, where I am the psychological spiritual seeker without, and they have abundance in the world of money?" I made an instantaneous decision to free myself from these roles that often occur in families. One person is the healthy, the next is the sick; one is spiritual, the other more material. Now although these are artificial divisions in some ways—as all the members of this family are both material and spiritual—it is the issue of identity, of what is us, therefore it all falls into place more or less unconsciously.

Seeing money as containing all kinds of unprocessed family issues is one key to becoming more conscious about money. This experience triggered the beginning of my launching out into the world of money. A journey of a broad scope, including learning how to make and keep money, as well as the understanding of how finances fit in with my psychology and spirituality, along with those of my family, clients, friends, and the world's issues.

Seventeen years ago, I had the most secure job I had ever held. I was director of a growing rural-based counseling agency, specializing in providing services to children and families. We had completed our first year and a half of a large and growing government awarded grant, and I finally had a regular salary I could count on. During this period of the grant, I had also separated from my wife. Considering she owned the house we had lived in together, I found myself suddenly needing to purchase my own house. I gathered all of my savings, put a down payment on a great house, and was looking forward to living in it and embarking on my new life as a single person. A few weeks after I closed on the house, I was informed that the funding on the grant was not going to be renewed.

I found myself instantaneously out of a job and now with huge financial obligations to meet. As we began to downsize the clinic, I felt obligated to pay vacation time to employees out of my own pocket, which was due them from when we had the grant, along with numerous other pressing expenses. Consequently I had ignored building my private practice, and therefore retained only four or five ongoing clients. I determined the only way I could survive was to rebuild my private practice, even though I knew it could take years to establish.

Then one night I dreamt that my teacher of Process-oriented Psychology, Dr. Arnold Mindell, and his father, whom I had never met, came to me. His father told me that I should relax around money; it was all going to work out. Without putting forth a lot of energy to build my practice, the phone began to ring. Suddenly I found myself seeing fifteen clients, and I was on my way to a full practice, which has remained solid ever since.

This experience was the original shock wave that eventually led to developing this book. Prior to experiencing that dream, I still boasted my anti-money views that were a holdover from my more radical, hippy days when I was in social work school. At that time in my life, I considered money to be a necessary evil that I would dabble in as long as it did not interfere with the rest of my life, including my spiritual life. Money was the furthest thing I could imagine relating to my spiritual interests.

I had always followed and worked with my dreams, and I considered dreams of money rather unimportant, except for this one. Why would this man, whom I had never met, appear in my dreams? Why was he so competent to predict that my practice would escalate, after it remained dormant for five years? That one dream challenged my view that money is just money and material. I had to consider the possibility that this miracle of clients materializing came from some other plane, and not just from my material efforts, for they had failed to build a practice previously.

Ten years later, I was talking with my father regarding money. At that point in our relationship, we were very close, and could discuss anything and everything, from dreams to money, politics, psychology and spirituality. My father was raised during the depression through which his family struggled financially. During his working life, he had worked relentlessly in the retail business, providing our family with a solid upper middle class existence, although we were never rich. Then, as he began to retire, my father became more and more skilled in investing in the stock market. He had brokers who actually called him for advice. He made quite a large sum of money, and when he told me how much, I was stunned.

One night, I had a dream that was as clear as the horizon on a bright summer's day. I dreamt the markets were going to crash within the next few months, and he should cash in all of his investments. When I shared this with him, he told me he would think about it, but felt that the markets were just starting to spiral upwards. This was shortly before the so-called dot.com crash of the markets in the year 2002. My father, along with many other retired people, lost the majority of what he had made. Looking back on these events, I recently realized that his decision to not follow my advice was partially based on the fact that I myself did not believe firmly enough in my own dreamwork to make a strong enough case to him.

I have since monitored my own dreams that take me in and out of the stock market, and as a result, I have become an even greater believer in the need to work with money consciously. I have learned to work with money as a concept that is far more significant and encompassing than that of the current worldview surrounding it. Money is an invaluable tool for us along our path of personal and spiritual growth. Money provides a motivation, a reason and a way to follow our profound inner wisdom, helping us deepen and unfold that wisdom, as we learn that our connection and ability to make money come are not just based on outer efforts but deep inner experiences.

In the first half of this book, I describe the wisdom of specific spiritual traditions, and I explain how Process-oriented

Psychology teaches us to work with issues around money. In the second part of this book, I discuss the distinct methods I have developed in working with money favoring dreams, in concert with additional approaches.

I genuinely believe that people can learn how to utilize their dreaming realms to facilitate making money in the stock market, along with other investments as well. My book follows this format. Following the dreaming process is complicated, as we need to be aware of when enough is enough, including embracing hard times as part of our development or path, and exercising our wealth in order to serve others.

My journey took me from being a man who never bothered to balance his check books to someone who spent four hours a day or more day trading in the stock market, in the midst of having a full therapy practice and teaching schedule. I made money during periods when the professional traders told me they were all losing. This book investigates what I have learned, and the questions I have that I am still exploring. As my dreams guided me in and out of the stock market, I began to rethink my deep-rooted attitude that money, spirituality, and the world of dreams and mysticism were altogether separate. I was sensitive to the myriad of theories that exclaim that money and spirit are connected, but I had not experienced it strongly enough to believe it. When I had no money at all, my dreams showed me the way to make the money I needed. When I became addicted to the stock market, and while I was making money, I began to see other parts of my life begin to fall apart. It was my dreams that told me when and how to get out.

In this book, I survey the details of the processes of how I learned to do this, and the techniques I am currently exploring in examining the realms of finance. Furthermore, I traverse welcoming and maintaining the desire for acquiring money, without becoming trapped in a way that could wound other and more important parts of my life.

Money causes happiness as well as suffering. I have met beggars on the streets of India who talked of their joy, and, in contrast, people with so many millions of dollars who were miserable. And yet, I am well aware that money can ease the suffering of many people. This book looks at how to have a positive relationship with money that reduces suffering of individuals, couples, families, and the world. Bringing awareness into financial lives is a stunning project that I am delighted to be a part of.

If I were to summarize the different books I read on applying spiritual traditions to the world of money, the central theme supports a middle road which embraces and connects the material life and spiritual life, and brings awareness to both. We will look specifically at what these different spiritual approaches bring to this issue.

The variety of psychology I practice and teach, Process-oriented Psychology, or Process Work as it is called, carries the equivalent emphasis on awareness. However, the Process Work methods I introduce to this topic of finances include unique approaches toward the same goals of awareness.

We examine the world of dreaming, which includes both our night dreams and our waking dreamlike experiences, always keeping in mind the question of how to deal with the world of money. We consider the central question of how to reveal what each of our individual paths has to do with money, and what that central Self—sending us our dreams—is asking of us in the money realm. From this point, we ascertain the ways to follow our deepest wisdom and guidance in the area of money, and utilize this wisdom to navigate what appears to be the polarities of spirituality; self-development on one side, and money and material achievement on the other side. We discover not only what our deepest selves derive from money, but what money teaches us about our deepest natures.

It is important to explore all of these aspects in terms of how our individual relationship to finances is partially determined by social issues, and by how our individual actions can contribute to or help resolve social issues and world problems. Part of the purpose of this book is to furnish the reader with concepts of how Process-oriented work can improve money issues. I have often said that good therapy means the client gets help with their money issues. I will express several stories of clients who made a great deal of money from decisions made in therapy sessions.

The exercises and stories I convey assist the reader in examining and navigating their money issues. However, a key point of Process Work is to enable each person to follow his or her own unique process around money. The path I advocate, following my dreaming, goes directly against the guidance of what almost all financial advisers would support. I have followed this direction partially because I have over thirty years of experience in psychological work. Through this work I have had access to other process workers, including Dr. Arnold Mindell, the founder of this work, to help me navigate the often tricky financial waters by using my dreaming process.

This financial tool of navigating one's investments is not for everyone. I also consult with traditional financial advisers. I highly recommend speaking with a traditional financial advisor prior to taking any significant financial risks, as well as a "financial dream advisor" trained in Process Work or similar methods. Even with all of these resources, keep in mind that even the experts do often get burned in the financial world, and there are no guarantees other than if you keep your eyes open, you may learn a great deal about the world of money and about yourself. The true goal of this work is not to make money, but to explore who you are, how the realm of money helps you wake up to who you are at your essence, and what your purpose is for being on this Earth.

Let's begin by looking at some of what the wise voices from various religious and spiritual traditions are saying in regard to the issues around the awareness of money. Money can certainly be a trap in terms of our spiritual growth, but can also be a fantastic place to struggle and wake up to our true natures.

I.
Spiritual Traditions and Money

| CHAPTER 1 |

Wisdom from the East

Fame or self: Which matters more?

Self or wealth: Which is more precious?

Gain or loss: Which is more painful?

He who is attached to things will suffer much.

He who saves will suffer heavy loss.

A contented man is never disappointed.

He who knows when to stop does not
find himself in trouble.

He will stay forever safe.

Lao Tse, in the Tao Te Ching,
translated by Gua-Fu Feng and Jane English (1972, p.44).

Lao Tse, the master of saying it all in a few words, introduces the central themes of this book in his passage. In an age of materialism, can we find an approach to money that is in the Tao, which is in harmony with nature? How do we reach the state of non-attachment that Lao Tse refers to, and how can we believe in a culture that so highly values accumulating more and more—to the point where the one who knows how to stop is the one who is safe? Let's explore the valued guidance and wisdom we can glean in this area from ancient and modern wisdom.

Buddhist Thinking and Money

There are different Buddhist traditions, and of course within these traditions are different schools of Buddhist thought. In this chapter, I examine what contemporary writers are saying about Buddhism and money. I initiate with writers who express Buddhism in an easily understandable format for Westerners.

In *Mindfulness and Money*, the Buddhist Path of Abundance, the authors Kulanada and Domonic Houlder express that we will learn from them the secret of financial peace. Of course what we do with this secret is up to us. They articulate that the path of renunciation of the world and money is one Buddhist path, but certainly not the only one. They quote Anguttara Kikaya II when they convey that the ideal life is to live "with robes sufficient to protect the body and alms food for the body's needs, taking just these, as a bird on the wing flies only with the load of its wings."(2002, p.7)

However, they explain that the householder was the second part of the Buddhist life, and "The Buddha's teachings were meant to transform anyone's life, regardless of lifestyle."(p.7) In fact, what follows is a quote from Buddha on a generous man or woman of great wealth."His case is like that of the beautiful lake I spoke of, but now it lies near a village or town where people can draw water and drink from it, bathe in it, or make any use for it for any other purpose. His riches go to enjoyment, not to waste."(2002, p.9)

These authors attempt to specifically apply these principles to Buddhism in the West. Later I will talk in detail about Process-oriented Psychology and concepts of rank and power. Buddha addresses these as well. In Process Work, we would describe this man Buddha refers to above with his position as having great social rank. He has money, wealth and other forms of consensus reality, daily living power. However, he uses this rank for the benefit of not only himself, but others as well. This is a key element in Buddhist and Process Work thinking. This concept expresses that being without money is not the goal of a spiritual life, but it is what you do with your life and your energy, which is reinforced again and again in many of these different approaches.

Kulanada and Dominic convey this message through talking about basic principles of Buddhism. They offer, "Money will not make your life complete. In fact, nothing will."(2002, p.13) They apply other basic principles of Buddhism as they relate to money. First, they talk about the illusion of the permanent self, explaining that, "Our self, then, is a temporary pattern that holds together for an alarmingly short time."(2002, p.15) The two continue, "We'll do our best to prevent change with anything at our disposal. We'll use money to pile up possessions around us to get a sense of permanence and security, like Egyptian pharaohs who hope to find immortality by building pyramids."(2002, p.15)

The second illusion discussed is that of our having a separate self. Kulanada and Dominic clearly state this is an illusion: "That's because the more we make things ours, as opposed to anyone else's, the more we reinforce the painful sense of separateness from other human beings and the world. It's the very sense of being separate that leaves us feeling incomplete."(2002, p.16)

The final illusion that we need to face is the illusion of the substantial self. They say that we talk about our position, our social rank, and our money to fix this sense of identity. However, "The reality is that there are no limits to what we are: there's an endless flux of changing processes that can't be contained by a particular identity.

Clinging to a particular identity makes us miss out so much of life that we're left feeling incomplete."(2002, p. 17) All of these illusions of the little "self" are presented in this book in the context of our use of money as a tool to reinforce this little "self," which does not enhance our deeper needs for meaning and connection to self, other, and the world.

Kulanada and Dominic's remedy for using money to fill this incompleteness is to live abundantly."To avoid the total impoverishment and to live abundantly, the challenge is to reverse our reactive, deluded response to our sense of incompleteness, and use our money to help us to do so."(2002, p.18)

By abundance, they suggest how "Buddhist practitioners have accomplished in crafting a creative relationship with money. You'll start to uncover your own destination: becoming more aware of your purpose in getting money and spending it."(2002, p. 21) Remarkable. They said a key word here, we must work on our relationship to money, and in that, money isn't just an object but also a process, a relationship process.

There is one other central concept they communicate from Tibbetan Buddhism that I would like to introduce in detail, which is that of the Wheel of Life. This wheel is divided into six worlds, and they present the issues around money in each of these worlds. First, they cover the animal world. This includes signs of our minds at the animal state. Their interpretation of animals and this level of life reflect a view towards animals that, in my opinion, puts them down and lacks understanding into the high levels of consciousness some animals display.

Their descriptions are geared toward upper middle class experiences, and yet can be applied in some way to all of us. They discuss moving fluidly between these worlds, and not being identified with just one. Their signs for the animal world are as follows:

- We're stuck in the same rut, doing a job that means little to us, spending eight hours a day, forty-eight weeks a year watching the clock and killing time.

- We spend each Saturday afternoon walking down the same supermarket aisles, putting the same items in our baskets as we did last week and the week before and the week before that, irrespective of price or quality, regardless of what goes into them and what effect they have on us and our environment.

- So as long as we meet our bills, with a little over, we're happy. Because what else can you expect from life? (2002, p.30)

The next realm is that of hungry ghosts."The hungry ghosts are driven by neurotic craving. Neurotic because the craving they experience is often the displaced desire for something else—something they are not consciously aware of. Wanting affection, not knowing how best to go about getting it, they crave chocolate instead."(2002, p. 30) Put in simple terms, they describe the land of addictions, including money addictions. We will discuss money addictions in a separate chapter later in the book.

They say that we become hungry ghosts when:

- We buy things, not because we need them or because we'll need them later and the price is reduced, but just because we need to buy something, anything almost.

- We try to control our spending but splurge on luxuries almost against our own wishes.

- We're suddenly obsessed with having a new bathroom or a new car (even though our current one is still running fine), or another dinner service, or an obscure kitchen gadget we saw advertised once, and we can't rest and can't think of anything else until we get it.

- We become preoccupied with our savings, checking the balance every week, not giving or spending more than we absolutely have to, piling up money purely for its own sake.(2002, p. 31)

Next are the hell worlds."Buddhism recognizes a number of different hell worlds whose occupants experience continuous torture and all kinds of deprivation, but none of these worlds lasts forever. There is no Buddhist equivalent of eternal damnation."(2002, p. 32)

Signs of being in the hell worlds include:

- We're trapped in painful jobs that we'd do anything to escape.

- We're bullied and harassed at work but can't quit.

- Our work generates intense levels of anxiety and tension that we cannot dispel.

- We're driven to keep going in our work purely out of fear of poverty. (2002, p. 32)

The next realm is that of the jealous-gods."According to Buddhist legend, the jealous-gods are constantly engaged in warlike struggle with the gods for the possession of the wish-fulfilling tree."(2002, p.32) This is the realm of competition and aggression, absolutely driven people, and "the pursuit of wealth, fame, and power."(2002, p. 33)

Here are the signs they describe that indicate these realms:

- We deviously maneuver for a promotion at work at the expense of our co-workers.

- We live to advance our own cause or that of our firm.

- We use anger and our ability to inspire fear to get what we want, especially from those beneath us in the hierarchy at work.

- We want something because we hate the idea of someone else having what we don't.

- We use our sexuality to manipulate others at work.

- We are preoccupied with our relative status.

- We buy things for the sake of demonstrating our status and power. (2002, p. 34)

The next realm is the world of the gods."According to Buddhist teachings, one of the difficulties people can have in the god world is that although it is a world of refined enjoyment, the gods tend to not do very much; their enjoyment tends to be rather passive." (2002, p. 34-35) It is easy to become complacent in this state. In this world, for example, the authors say that many Buddhists feel that inherited wealth comes from good past life karma, but the challenge is then to use one's wealth in this life for the benefit of others. This again corresponds with the Process Work concept "Have your rank and use it for the benefit of all."

The following are signs of money behavior in this world:

- We shop with care and discrimination, buying things only for their genuine aesthetic qualities and not only because of fashion or passing whims.

- Our work itself gives rise to calm, refined mental states.

- We make spending choices that genuinely uplift us, saving to buy really good seats at the theater for example, or for a trip to one of the cultural capitals of Europe.(2002, p. 36)

Finally, we have the human world."The human world is marked by a kind of balance. In it, we experience a certain amount of pleasure and certain amount of pain. One of its chief characteristics is that it is a world in which we have a degree of self-awareness and in which we are able to make significant choices." (2002, p. 37)

Here are the signs of being in this state of mind:

- Our financial lives give rise to a mix of pleasure and pain, but we're not overwhelmed by the pain of it or intoxicated by the pleasure. Instead we continue to make reasonable, clear, informed choices.

- We enjoy our work and our leisure.

- We form good friendships at work.

- We're able to forget about money for long periods of time.

- Our work allows us to grow and develop.

- We experience twinges of anxiety in relation to money, but we act appropriately and they pass.

- We buy what we need and we don't feel guilty about it.

- We don't obsess about what we want to buy next.

- We use our money to come closer to our families, friends, neighbors, the community, and the wider world.

- What we have is enough.

I believe the majority of us would agree that we would feel a great deal of satisfaction to spend most of our time in the human realm.

It is interesting to note that most of the methods of working on money in *Mindfullness and Money* are what I would call more mainstream interventions; that is, these methods deal with bringing awareness to how much we spend and how much we give. They also provide dialogue around the amount of time we allocate towards love, people, recreation, and other mediums that occupy our time and thought in addition to money. There are many excellent books written on the daily level of life that clarify tracking your expenditures, understanding your time, developing budgets, defining goals, and suggestions for maintaining and keeping your eyes wide open around money. The authors summarize what they consider a proper attitude by quoting the Japanese poet Buson:

'What you want to acquire, you should acquire by any means. What you want to see, even though it is with difficulty, you should see. You should not let it pass, thinking there will be another chance to see it or acquire it. It is quite unusual to have a second chance to materialize your desire.' (2002, p.232)

I am including in the section on Buddhism in this book, the work of Jacob Needleman, and his book, *Money and the Meaning of Life*. While it is not strictly regarding Buddhism, his thinking is very close to Buddhist texts. Needleman succeeds in outlining what he sees as a middle way around money issues.

Although I would have liked to cover the entire depth of Needleman's insight, I examined only the key issues that he presents. His common sense approach explores several key points. One of his main points is that we have confused money as a means and money as an end. This is one of the reasons we have become so attached to money. Without warning it takes over and itself becomes the goal, rather than that of using money to foster important life and societal goals. He brings the differences in means and ends into the discussion of giving. One of the strongest lines in his book is the question, "Is there a quality of awareness that is itself something we receive as a gift, and is there a quality of awareness that we can give to our world without needing to take anything?"(1991, p.XXI)

He continues to examine with us our general awareness of money."It shows us that almost all of our life with money proceeds without our conscious interaction, without our accompanying ourselves." (1991, p. XXIV) He continues with, "that such an exercise (becoming aware) can show us that the values we actually put into practice, as measured by what we spend money on, do not correspond to what we imagine about ourselves. This is therefore an exercise in the practice of self-sincerity, without which it will not be possible to develop a new and freer attitude toward money or toward life itself."(1991, p. XXIV)

Needleman emphasizes awareness, which is also the key to Process-oriented Psychology. He continues, explaining, "The present book is in many ways no more a discourse on this power of money to make things real. It is a power that many people regard with distaste. It is the argument of this book, however, that if we are seeking something in ourselves and in our common life that is both deeply meaningful and unshakably real, then in this time and place, in this culture that shapes us all, we have no choice but to take very seriously the power money has not only to seduce or frighten us, but to show us what we can develop in ourselves that can never be bought or sold at any price." (1991, p.XXVI)

This is very close to the Buddhist idea of cutting through all illusions to what is real, and then being conscious of how we engage in that realness. Needleman speaks of how many books are available on the quest to have money, but how few there are on the quest for linking money and meaning. My book joins his book in this journey. He states, "I am saying that money—that extraordinary device whose origins we shall soon discuss—now plays an unprecedented powerful role in our inner and outer lives, and that any serious search for self-knowledge and self-development requires that we study the meaning that money actually has for us." (1991, p.3)

This statement completely captured my attention. Until the past year or so, I had always thought that studying money was a hindrance, a divergence from my spiritual path. Needleman says not only is it not a hindrance, but it is a requirement for spiritual advancing. He explains that we have to look at all aspects of our lives: "Love and hatred, eating and sleeping, safety and danger, work and rest, marriage, children, fear, loneliness, friendship, knowledge, art, health, sickness and death. The money factor is a determining element in all of these—sometimes plainly visible, sometimes blended into the whole fabric like a weaver's dye." (1991, p. 3)

If this wasn't enough to contemplate, he then continues to endorse that we must take this out into the world."If we broaden our vision and consider the whole condition of the human family, we see the same penetration of the money factor into every facet of the crisis of the modern world: war, social injustice, the oppression of peoples and classes, crime in all its violent and nonviolent forms, our dying natural environment."(1991, p.3) Now we are getting somewhere. Our relationship to money is part of what organizes our world, and we must begin living with our eyes wide open about such a huge influence that often runs like the computer program in the background.

This goes along with the Zen and Process Work notions of waking up to the here and now realities of what is in front of you, and not simply operating on automatic pilot.

Needleman proceeds to outline the depth of this problem of consciousness around money. He rationalizes, it is more than just a psychological or social problem which one strives to correct in advance of attending to question the spiritual. It has become the key to understanding the great purpose of human life and what precisely, prevents us from participating in that great purpose. Because money is a problem that enters into the whole of human life, it cannot be dealt with in a piecemeal fashion on the level at which it presents itself—pragmatically, psychologically, or moralistically—any more than one can escape from prison by visiting the prison psychologist or social worker and improving conditions inside the prison walls. (1991, p.4)

Needleman talks about all of this in terms of awakening to our essential nature. He enlightens, "The aim is nothing more nor less than to sacrilege the moral question. This does not mean making money itself is sacred. It means finding the precise place of money at the heart of the most important undertaking of our lives—the search to become what we are meant to be in the service of the greatness that calls to every man or woman on the endangered earth." (1991, p. 16) He shares of how in all great spiritual and religious traditions there is this moment of awakening out of illusion; what greater place to work on this than in the arena of money?

Needleman attempts to bridge the gap, using the rest of his book to compare different religions and their attempts to unite the outer world of materialism with the inner world of meditation, prayer and reflection. He talks about the need to develop fluidity between these worlds so that we don't get stuck in either. He explains that the problem is that the outer world concerns of materialism have come to dominate the inner life."It has come to seem so real not only because there are no longer strong enough experiences of the inner world, but also because there are no longer conscious experiences of the two worlds together." (1991, p.161)

If I could summarize Needleman's book in one sentence, it would be in his referring to the deep mystical parts of religion. He says, "It follows of necessity that man must be aware of both movement, both directions that he has with him which can be in contact with God and money, good and evil, being and nonbeing."(1991, p. 162) Thus, our enlightenment around money means nothing less than the development of our whole self.

In terms of money, "Man needs to study himself with such diligence and concern that the very act of self-study becomes as vivid and intense as the desires and fears he is studying. The truth shall set you free. Not because it will give you explanations, but because the conscious experience of the truth, even when the truth is hellish, is itself space and light and contact with a higher world." (1991, p. 171) He says if you study yourself meaningfully and deeply, you will arrive at a place where you must confront the split between the desire for God and the desire for money and material comfort, and that it is the awakening process that occurs by facing this contradiction.

Needleman explains that in Hebrew this is called "a broken heart," and later, during the turning point in the great monastic communities of the Christians, it was called "tears and sorrow." It was what Solomon of legend experienced in his years of exile. Today in our present era, we may speak of it, giving it an entirely new dimension of power and consciousness. (1991, p.171) Needleman describes this awakening as a requirement to an authentic spiritual path, and a way of life that reflects this state. People must study themselves and not run away from money.

If you examine yourself profoundly, you will arrive at this place that Needleman describes. He goes on to say, "The aim is to have the experience of truth become as interesting as money and things. More interesting! Nothing could be more practical than deepening the experience of truth." (1991, p.182) Needleman says that this awakening requires an authentic spiritual path, and once on this path, personal gain and giving to others are intimately connected.

Needleman affirms beautifully the challenge we face. His description of the non-stop, intense studying of oneself instantly reminded me of my trip into the stock market. I have rarely had to study myself with such intensity, including those aspects of myself that are uncomfortable to examine, involving my more addictive tendencies, the places I try to fill where I feel empty, and other such painful places I discuss in Chapter 8 on money addictions. My association with the stock market forced me into this severe inner examination.

I want to end this discussion of Needleman with his quoting of Rumi on who is at your funeral, and how serious our daily living is to our eternal self. Rumi speaks, "Three companions for you? Number one, what you own. He won't even leave the house for some danger you might be in. He stays inside. Number two, your good friend. He at least comes to the funeral. He stands and talks at the gravesite. No further. The third companion, what you do, your work, goes down into death to be there with you, to help. Take deep refuge with that companion, beforehand." (1991, p. 288-289) Keep in mind I opened this book with the line from an old movie, "Your money or your life." Rumi offers his own version on how to solve this, with awareness of what is truly lasting and important, one's life work.

CHAPTER 2

Kabbalah and Money

Writing on Jewish mystical approaches to money provides profound wisdom and includes insights into the social issue of anti-Semitism. One of my main goals in writing this chapter is to identify and clarify the roots of the Jewish attitude toward money, and to distinguish this reality from the prejudices and projections that have been directed toward the Jewish people.

For centuries, Jews have been negatively projected in the money arena. From the beginning in the Middle Ages, the Jews were restricted to working in society's most hated jobs, such as tax collectors and money lenders. In the years following, they were blamed for being too focused and excessively involved with money. It became easier to project onto the Jews such shallow desires and attachments around money, than it was for individuals to consciously face their own relationship with and aspirations for money. So I ask each of you who reads this, whether Jewish or not, to please be aware of the anti-Semitic feelings this chapter may evoke, and to use your awareness to break through this century-old collective prejudice.

Rabbi Nilton Bonder, in his book, *Kabbalah of Money, Jewish Insights on Giving, Owning, and Receiving*, introduces us to the wonderful world of Kabbalistic principles and money. I was immediately struck by how similar the principles that Rabbi Bonder discusses are with the Buddhist principles offered forth in the previous chapters. He starts his book by saying that, "a man shows his character in three ways; by his cup (that is his appetite), his pocket (his relationship to money) and his anger. Here we will concern ourselves with the "pocket" and how much we reveal of ourselves when dealing with it. In everyone's pocket, questions of survival and its boundaries come to light—questions related to excess, ownership, and insecurity. (1996, p.1)

He continues by saying, "We can't get from the heart to the pocket without looking at life as a whole and all its meanings. How we relate to our pocket reveals who we are and where we stand within the immense Market of values that we call reality."(1996, p.1-2) This is in one sentence a summary of is entire book: that in our relationship to money lies, at its core, our essential being. We can project onto Jews and others in a prejudiced fashion, but this will not help us to know our totality.

Bonder discusses these prejudices when he talks about how, "In a way, Jews are indispensable to the collective memory of the West. Upon them the West projects many of its social fantasies, as well as many of civilization's sublimated and repressed experiences, which tend to manifest in those perceived in being "other." (1996, p.3) He continues to describe how far off these prejudiced statements are from the reality of Jewish values and teachings.

Rabbi Bonder tells us that through this exploration of money, he is taking us into the realms of money, "a journey into the shadows cast by money on emotional and spiritual dimensions. We shall look at our exchanges in such a way that the dark shadow of our souls is cast off from money, come to accept our human limits of wealth."(1996, p.5-6) He says money "arises from the human desire for justice and the hope for a better world."(1996, p.6)

Rabbi Bonder tells a story that illustrates this point. He talks of a rabbi who was once honored by being allowed to witness both purgatory and heaven. In both places, people were seated before an unbelievable feast of food, yet because their elbows were inverted somehow, they couldn't bend their arms and bring food to their mouths. The only difference between the two was that in heaven, people fed each other.

Accordingly, this model of everyone being fed and the desire for justice (as mentioned above) are adjoining to the true spirit and essence of the teachings of a Jewish approach to money. Jews are to take poverty—and its elimination—seriously. In the Midrash, the collection of Jewish writings of the rabbis, there is a teaching from Exodus Rabbah 31:14 that captures the importance of working for the goal of eliminating poverty.

Bonder quotes from Exodus Rabbah, "Nothing in the universe is worse than poverty; it is the most terrible of sufferings. A person oppressed by poverty is like someone who carries on his shoulders the weight of the whole world's sufferings. If all the pain and the suffering of this world were placed on one scale and poverty on the other, the balance would tilt towards poverty." (1996, p.14) He continues to explain that the answer to this suffering is yshuv olam, what he calls the "settling of the world." Each of us is responsible for increasing the level of well-being upon the planet.

The recommended formula is to increase abundance without creating scarcity, and to improve the quality of life for all beings. Our job isn't necessarily to hold ourselves back, but instead to move forward, and encourage our own and others' development of abundance in a way that is win-win. If I gain by hurting you, this isn't sustainable, but if I gain and in doing so, help my neighbor to have a better life as well, then I have followed the life giving and sustaining teachings of the tradition.

Another key concept to consider is that of free will and *segulah*. Free will comes from consciousness and is connected with effort, while *segulah* comes from the soul and is something we are not able to consciously alter. He continues to explain, "According to the rabbis, we all carry with us inbred movements of livelihood: some are active and represent the sum of our conscious efforts; others are passive, like a "treasure" hidden inside our soul, which emerges in the form of luck, say, or a knack for business."(2001, p. 30)

The previous quote becomes fundamental when I begin explaining how to use our dreams for our financial life, and how the process helps connect us to this soul level. Also, he introduces here for me, one of the central keys relating to the style of approach I will describe later in this book as part of Process-oriented Psychology.

Similar to Kabbalah, this is a heaven and earth approach, which states that whatever we do in the material world is a combination of effort as well as non-doing, of action as well as inaction. As much as right action is important, so is this deep listening to the soul, or we become more like chickens running around with our heads cut off. Bonder quotes Rebbe Nachman, "Nonsuccess is a momentary expression of parnasha, livelihood. The greater cycle —of segulah, treasure— remains unaltered. If we give this cycle time, it will recompose itself."(2001, p.33) Therefore, segulah gets you further than correct decisions. Seguallah can be transformed into wealth. Quantum physicists would refer to this Seguallah as potential energy.

Rabbi Bonder then leads us into a Kabbalistic understanding of the bigger picture behind momentary wealth. From an immediate perspective, we might think this or that person doesn't deserve wealth, but these things can only be understood over the course of evolution of the soul over many, many lifetimes. Many Kabbalists believe in reincarnation, thereupon what happens in the moment is simply an expression of this one moment in the context of the flow of many lifetimes. He helps us to understand our fate regarding money by looking at our financial lives from the perspective of the four different worlds. He starts with the world of Asiyyah, which is the world of consensus reality, and the material world. Then there is Yetzira, which he calls the emotional world, which is where the inner treasure I have referred to earlier lies. This is still a revealed world that we can see, equating to someone who has a green thumb or Midas's touch, enabling one to turn things into gold.

In the world of Beriah, the spiritual world, we deal with issues of merit, of not only what is our merit but the spiritual lineage of our ancestors as well. He compares this realm to the Buddhist idea of positive karma, assessing ideas of merit and of things incidentally working out for someone, as to mean the person has positive karma. When I begin to go deeper into my own story around money, I will talk about this realm of addressing financial issues that have existed through many generations.

Finally, in the world of Atzilut, we are in the realm of the infinite and our connection to the infinite. In Atzilut, we act solely because some action is coming through us; we are a channel for experiences, carrying no expectations of personal gain.

Whether or not people formally identify with these worlds, we nevertheless still experience them. For example, if we are investing in the stock market, many of us track the day-by-day changes, the reports, and many other aspects of consensus reality. It is rare however, that I come across a trader who will not admit to the role that intuition plays, and how if they are open to it, this intuition also comes in through dreams and in dreamlike experiences.

Traders often share that they just seem directed to do something, to buy or to sell, as if a hand is guiding their actions. The point is that issues of luck, superstitions, and all these other forces that enter into the non-rationale parts of our money life show that we are impacted in our financial lives by more than rationale forces. The mystic or the Process Worker focuses and explores these other worlds, while others may not notice them and just feel buffeted around by some kind of random universe. Rabbi Bonder quotes the famous mystic, the Baal Shem Tov, and his beliefs that "what happens to our daily, material lives comes from the realms way beyond simple coincidence."

Modern psychologists also join in support of Rebbe Nachman and the Baal Shem Tov. Jung's concept of synchronicity, of meaningful coincidence, harmonizes flawlessly with the teachings offered by these mystics. As we get deeper into this book, I will explore the views of Mindell, the founder of Process-oriented Psychology, and his theory that life is twenty-four hour dreaming. One of the key concepts of Process-oriented Psychology is the importance of transcending the causal thinking that says, "This leads to that, that leads to this," and that "you can find a reason or cause for everything." Going beyond this paradigm guides us into exploring the realms of dreams, myths and dreamlike phenomena, where life has a much deeper meaning than we can generally recognize. From here, we can then connect with Earth-based wisdom and the wisdom of the universe.

This is the manner of deeper meaning that the Baal Shem Tov clarifies. The Baal Shem Tov describes perceiving subtle realities. It is from this level of complex realities that we must look at our money situations in life; not simply the consensus reality, or bank account level. Again, this substantiates Rabbi Bonder's views that we must also be careful not to create anti-wealth, which again comes from the idea that if we create wealth at the cost of the whole, rather than benefiting the whole, we actually have lost and not gained in the larger picture.

Bonder calls this an ecological view of wealth, in which it is crucial to ascertain that we do not benefit in consensus reality by increasing our wealth whilst opposing our deepest nature and the will of the universe. In doing so, therefore, we are actually contributing to creating more poverty. This key issue became a challenge for me when I started to get more and more involved in the stock market. I had to learn to balance my financial well-being with my health (as I got less and less sleep) and my relationship (as I spent less and less focused time there), in addition to setting time aside for my spiritual work, my social action volunteering and my therapy practice. Finding myself unable to increase the money without eventually sacrificing too many other realms, I eventually left trading. It is very difficult to train ourselves for success in most of our major ventures in this world while maintaining a more holistic and balanced view. We are trained by society to be more and more focused and specialized, especially where certain materialistic values seem to trump and marginalize so many other important values.

One of the implications of this view is that we need an impeccable sense of timing around money, particularly of when to hold on and when to let go. I will return to this point several times throughout this book, as it is one of the central points of my focus. Following this more dreamlike, spiritual path to money also means following it wherever it goes. If the path leads to being very materialistic and making lots of money, that may be easy to follow, but how about when the path tells us "that is enough," or "give some of it away.?"

Rabbi Bonder says it like this."As Moishe the Kabbalist used to say, when something is yours, nobody can take it from you. And when something is no longer yours, it can be dangerous to hold on to. Learning to enjoy ownership up until almost the last minute is what distinguishes the true hero, the master of the non-consumerist era that will one day be inaugurated in our world." (2001, p.96) He continues to explain, "Knowing how to let go at the right time, not a moment too soon nor a moment too late, is a sacred art." (p.96)

Consider, it is Lao Tse who shares the same basic truth in the quote presented at the start of this book: "He who is attached to things will suffer much. He who saves will suffer heavy loss. A contented man is never disappointed. He who knows when to stop does not find himself in trouble. He will stay forever safe."

Rabbi Bonder writes a great deal about the path of tzedakah. Tzedakah is a Jewish custom traditionally associated with charity, yet Bonder clarifies that this is a translation problem into English, and the true meaning of tzedakah is justice. He says, "Tzedakah is of fantastic importance to the Market. It is one of its intelligent operators, translating our attitudes into a desire for enrichment of the comos."(2001, p.64) Tzedakah ties us to economic justice."And if wealth doesn't seek to ameliorate poverty, then by definition, it impoverishes itself." (2001, p. 64)

This teaching is part of the larger, holistic perspective. Can I possibly focus on increasing my own wealth, and eliminating poverty at the same time? Too often, at least in modern America, this principle seems forgotten by the political leaders, who seem to favor the advancement of the wealthy at the cost of the poor.

Both in Kabbalah and in Process-oriented Psychology, which I will cover in great detail in the coming sections of this book, there is the foundational belief that out of the negative figures in our lives and in our dreams, there is energy, and lessons to be harvested. Rabbi Bonder talks about harvesting the energy, while learning the lessons of the thief. He talks of the great rabbi the Maggid of Meseritz, who took lessons from the thief, "perseverance, fraternity, courage, detachment, tolerance for frustration, and dedication are antidotes distilled from the very poison that harms the Market." (2001, p.91)

Like Buddhist thinking, the Kabbaalists emphasize knowing how to move through the ever-changing nature of life, along with the money markets. Rabbi Bonder says, "No one who has ever experienced livelihood in abundance or success in any area is immune to downfalls. On the contrary, the higher up we are, the more we must deposit as security for the moments of descent. We must make these deposits in riches of the soul so that during our falls, we may be warmed by faith in the recurring rise. We must learn to share enthusiasm over the fact that the wheel is turning, and not go into spirals of anguish because another fall is approaching." (2001, p.103-4)

Buddhists call this getting off the wheel. He also talks of how Rebbe Nachman used to say that we have to first go down in order to learn how to fight despair and rise up again. Rabbi Bonder says, "Blessed is the One who made fate like a wheel, for He gave the well a bottom and made it such that the strength of what rises supports whatever falls."(2001, p. 104)

Another key to living in the world of money is to know exactly what we want, and for what reasons. Rabbi Bonder continues to describe the great mystic, the Bal Shem Tov, who talked of how the saint, or tzaddik (a righteous person), isn't tied to the wheel of livelihood because "he is in fact, livelihood itself." (2001, p. 109) His teaching here is similar to the Buddhist idea of right livelihood that somehow the money just flows when we are in line with our true natures, and true purpose, and in service of the greater Beingness of the universe. He is describing this fluid place of making money without effort, doing what we love, and simultaneously continuing to serve the betterment of humanity.

The rabbi's view of luck, differs from "mazel" as it is said in Yiddish,The two concepts together address the central issue of what this book is about. He says, "Mazel is when a need leaves this dimension and goes into other worlds in search of livelihood. When it returns, it surfaces magically. Luck is the materialization of our livelihood when it comes from other worlds into the material dimension."(2001, p.144) Yes, this is what this book is focusing on, that money isn't just about effort, investment and knowledge, but is connected to the other unseen dimensions, and that these experiences can be cultivated and worked with to help enhance our lives and the lives of others.

In the next chapter, we look at Process-oriented Psychology, or Process Work as it is called—the method I am trained in, practice and teach—and how it deals with money. What follows is a quote from Rabbi Bonder, which is based on the same principles I will introduce in how Process Work emphasizes the importance of living our lives connected to not only the world of ordinary reality, but to the dreaming worlds. Rabbi Bonder talks about money in this same multi-world approach when he is discussing Rebben Nachman's teaching of making use of your gifts and treasures.

Bonder illustrates, "He was trying to point out to us the riches we have in the various worlds and that we don't know how to use. If you understand the interconnection between the various worlds of wealth, then you know the dangers of concentrating your wealth in one dimension only. And you'll discover that you can transfer these riches from one dimension to the other when necessary."(2001, p.142-3) One might interpret this to mean that money isn't just about working hard, investing and other consensus, daily world approaches to making ends meet. Instead, it also has to do with the realms of dreams, intuitions, and hunches and those things that catch our attention and flirt with our awareness.

In the second half of this book, I will share my own stories of working with my own and with my clients' dreams and deepest experiences that translate into the realm of money. Rabbi Bonder then follows this quote on the many worlds with portraying a story about a rabbi who had a dream, followed it, and found a treasure.

In Process Work, we talk about parallel worlds, a term that comes from quantum physics, that helps us to understand all of these worlds; these different dimensions are present at all times, and they parallel each other, meaning we have to learn how to travel between the worlds, and bring in information from one world to the other. Rabbi Bonder says, "Luck helps us to notice the existence of these parallel worlds of wealth. The great plus is that it surprises us. And we all need to be surprised in order to open our hearts to these other dimensions." (2001, p.148) He continues, saying that the energy that crosses these dimensions, which allows us to go between parallel worlds, is that of angels.

Rabbi Bonder goes on to warn about the entrapment of wealth. It is a bright light, but not to be confused with true wealth. True wealth must be connected with both the spiritual parallel worlds and the material wealth. I very much enjoyed Rabbi Bonder's view of the four worlds, and the different wealth in each world. In the world of action, the blessings are in material goods and what may safeguard you is responsible taxing. In Yetzirah, foundation, the wealth is treasure and what may safeguard it are acts of kindness. In the world of creation, wealth is merit, and what may safeguard it is being holy. Finally, in the highest world, emanation, where there are no longer polarities, there are no rewards, and all is done for its own sake. What protects this world is learning and study.

One idea is that when we convert into capital, when we draw money, it is like we are drawing from our Big Bank account of energy that the rabbis believed in as investments in potential energy that can be converted. We must invest in all dimensions, not just the material. Our interactions with others are part of our investment. Without multi-dimensional investing, we lose all our material investments, if not before, along with death."Our neighbor is our first goal in trying to join with the One."(2001, p.167)

Rabbi Bonder finishes by reminding us repeatedly that we cannot take material wealth with us, but only our consciousness that is reflected in our good deeds and our love of learning. For in the world to come, we will be in a constant time of learning and studying, that we are preparing for in this world. The love of learning reaches very deeply into the essence of our being, and Rabbi Bonder confirms this as traveling into the afterlife with us as well. It is part of our wealth that transcends this world.

Section II— Process Psychology, Money, and My Story

| CHAPTER 3 |

Process-Oriented Psychology and Dreaming Money

Basic Concepts

Process-oriented Psychology, founded by Dr. Arnold Mindell, is a unique approach that integrates individual, couples, family, and world work. A client could be an individual, couple, family, or two nations or ethnic groups in conflict. Process Work is many things: a therapy method, a conflict work method, an approach to meditation, and a way of life. Process Work also, for myself, became a pathway to discovering how to work with money. Here I will briefly introduce a selection of the main concepts of Process Work, in aims of making the interventions I recommend and the stories I tell easier for the reader to grasp. The following concepts arise from the theoretical background of Process Work.

A basic belief of process work is that nature expresses itself in a conscious and meaningful way. The therapist is seen as a facilitator and supporter of nature. Due to the fact that the therapist follows the process wherever it goes, at times she may appear to be a body worker, at times a family therapist, and at times a facilitator for a large group of 300 people or more. Regardless of context, the facilitator is committed to discovering and supporting the process with awareness. Therefore, when it comes to money, a Process-oriented approach follows the process wherever it goes—into loss, gain, wealth, poverty, and everything in between. This perspective says that we can follow nature also in how "green energy" the energy of money flows.

All Process Work practitioners share the viewpoint that nature is the all-inclusive force behind occurrences in our individual and collective lives. This approach assumes that within the force of nature there lies deep wisdom, and that our work as therapists and facilitators is to help ourselves and others stay in contact with this force. When I refer to "believing in nature," I refer to the Process Work philosophy that nature provides an inherent background wisdom that can be discovered and followed. Whatever happens to occur is considered meaningful, and this meaning reveals itself over time. My own work then has been to follow nature's path as She guides me through the complicated world of earning and investing money.

This "belief in nature" also includes the premise that inner and outer wisdom are interrelated. We can learn more of who we are by knowing what is happening in the world, and seeing how the world's issues are also our issues. We can begin to understand the world on a deeper level by finding its problems inside ourselves."Belief in nature" is a way of relating to the world through careful observation and through action that arises out of this new level of awareness.

For myself personally, it was an incredible struggle and eye opening experience to perceive nature behind the forces of the stock market, a public entity I had always assumed was as unnatural, or out of sync with nature, as possible.

Through delving into the financial world, I discovered that the same kind of awareness we apply to working on a dream, body problem, world conflict situation or relationship issue, we can administer in working with the issues of money.

Bringing more awareness into a situation provides a means to discover and follow the wisdom of nature. This means no longer simply following one part of ourselves as some program to either earn and accumulate or to self sabotage and not earn, continuing to lose money. It means to allow nature to show us the way to follow our own deep natural rhythms while addressing our money issues. This leads to sustainability rather than potential burnout and other such issues.

It is this background wisdom the Process Work facilitator hopes to discover—in fact, nature is the real facilitator, and the Process Worker's goal is simply to help guide people back to their connection with it. In the next chapter, I will describe how I found those same forces of nature behind what was driving me deeper and deeper into day trading, and how my becoming aware of them allowed me to make significant conscious choices about money and my life.

The philosophical roots of Process Work's belief in nature are found in Taoism. In *The Deep Democracy of Open Forums*, Arnold Mindell points to Taoism as a bedrock of Process Work."Process Work is based on an ancient Chinese belief in nature called Taoism, which includes all possible states of mind such as conflict and peace, stagnation and breakthrough… I understand Taoism to say that we should notice and observe nature, then be at peace with what is happening, be it conflict or rest." (2002, p. 6) I would add to this be it loss or gain, accumulating or divesting, working or resting.

In light of uncovering nature's presence in the money realms, we could specifically add to this quote "gain or loss in the financial worlds." If I had been unable to find this place of being at peace with whatever happens, I would have found myself in terrible trouble in my financial dealings. With this connection to the Tao, to the flow of whatever is happening, I found a way to navigate safely in and out of sensitive financial areas that can be potentially hazardous. My goal became following nature and no longer simply winning the accumulation game.

Dr. Amy Mindell, in *Metaskills*, discusses applying the belief in nature to clinical interventions:

> The Process Worker—like the ancient Chinese Taoist—tries to observe the spontaneous arrangements of nature and assist the client and herself to adjust to this changing flow. She does not have a program as to what to do with a client, but allows nature to instruct her… Like the Taoist, she assumes that everything is already present in the spontaneous manifestations of nature. She must simply adjust, interact with and assist nature's path. (1995, p. 59)

Whether working with a physical symptom, a relationship problem, or a large group conflict, the client and therapist try to follow nature as closely as possible, asking the basic question: What does nature want to happen? It is essential to apply this approach to the world of money. Although it may be easy for me to believe that I am following nature when I am making money, how about when I am losing it? Can I identify with the mind of a learner, who is growing whether losing or making money? What if nature tells me I am to be financially rich? How about if nature says that I have emphasized money enough, and should shift to other areas of my life? Can I follow Her there? Can I remember Her when I am attached and winning in the markets for example? How about when I am losing? Can I remember Her?

Prior to pulling myself out of the stock market, I made one last high stakes purchase. That last purchase cost me, in a few hours, most all of my profits from my entire career as a trader. Can I learn from such an experience, and understand it as part of my fate? When I made most of the money back and my dreams told me it was time to quit trading, could I follow this perception? All of these are questions I want to explore throughout the book.

Process Work integrates theories and techniques from a wide variety of sources. Mindell began to develop Process Work out of his observations of body symptoms. He began to study body issues in his patients when he visited them in hospital settings. Surprisingly, when he asked them what he could do with his hands to help them feel better, he discovered that they almost always wanted him to help them experience their symptoms even more. Mindell called this, "amplifying a symptom." His tremendous breakthrough came when he noticed that during work with clients' bodies, they often recalled and began talking about dreams; likewise, during dream work with clients, body experiences and symptoms emerged.

These observations led Mindell to the concept of the dreambody, the part of ourselves that is both dream and body simultaneously. Mindell eventually integrated the dreambody concept into relationships, extreme states, comas, art and creativity, and finally to group work. He found that not only individuals, but couples, families, and even cities have their own dream and mythical levels that cry out to be explored.

Mindell explains, "I have always been more interested in the ways in which dreams appear in various aspects of everyday reality than in the dream images themselves. Today it is clear to me that dreams are just one of the manifestations of 'the unconscious,' which I will call, from now on, 'the Dreaming.' I love Jung's term, 'the unconscious.' Nevertheless, in my imagination, today he [Jung] would prefer the term 'the Dreaming' because of its connection with Aboriginal Australians and with cultures that support simultaneous awareness of dreaming and wakeful consciousness." (2002, p.11) In my trading days I noticed I was starting to develop more indigestion. The indigestion was part of my body's feedback on the stress I was putting myself under. I couldn't just digest my food well. I was not doing well digesting the change in emphasis on my path from being that of a therapist and conflict worker to that of a day trader.

In *River's Way*, Mindell talks about Process Work's integration of many body-oriented traditions:

> For example, if the process worker (kinesthetically) amplifies a client's repeated tendency to stretch, yawn and groan, specific postures from ancient yoga and modern bioenergetics appear as part of the fluid process of events. If he works verbally with the repressed sexual life of a theologian he will soon find proprioceptive experiences which encourages the client to let himself enjoy pleasure along the lines of Wilhelm Reich. If he works with the slow kinesthetic activity of the paralyzed person, processes mirroring the work of Feldenkrais appear. A shy woman who visualizes violent

> encounters may have a process which switches from fantasy to violent interaction which one can find in restructuring processes used by Ida Rolf. A client who uses her fingers to explain a migraine is indicating the specific proprioceptive process typical of acupuncture.
>
> If the Process Worker amplifies the tendency of a dreamer to speak to a particular dream figure during a dream report, then he develops a type of Black Elk dream ritual, psychodrama or active imagination. A Process Worker observing the breathing of a homosexual man trying to cope with sexual excitement may rediscover Taoist Alchemy's transformation of energies. A young person burdened by social conventions and parental complexes who tends to "lose his mind in order to come to his senses" unravels the Gestalt psychology of Fritz Perls. A reflective woman in need of exact information about her behavior and conflict with her husband can create transactional analysis. (1985, p. 8)

Mindell considers all these different approaches as aspects of Process Work that will emerge spontaneously as a client's signals are followed. While Process Work builds on all of these traditions, the practitioner does not learn hundreds of approaches but instead follows each approach as it appears instinctively in the work. This way of following the practice in order to discover the method is also found in yoga, where certain schools say that as practitioners become more advanced, they should follow their bodies, and yoga postures will emerge spontaneously. I am saying here that as people in their financial dealings become more advanced, they don't just follow their broker's advice and whatever other people are saying, but they learn to follow their bodies and dreams as their reliable and tremendous sources of information.

Process Work theory and methods are based on awareness, and consider building awareness to be more important than achieving a certain result. Mindell comments, "Awareness can change a painful situation into an enriching one. To prevent violence, we need to become aware of feelings and the pain... awareness can lead to new relationships, new dances." (2002, p. 7)

A Process-oriented therapist or facilitator follows nature by focusing on the signals that are present in client and therapist, facilitator and group. In *The River's Way*, one of Mindell's earliest works on Process Work theory, he defines process: "I use the word process to refer to changes in perception, to the variation of signals experienced by an observer. The observer's personality determines which signals he picks up, which he is aware of and which he identifies himself with and therefore which he reacts to." (1985, p. 11)

These signals appear and are followed through specific perceptual channels such as vision, audition, feeling, and movement. Process Work is feedback-oriented. The therapist or facilitator makes interventions by following signals, and then looks for feedback. This approach of following nature contrasts with theories that emphasize understanding certain theoretical constructs or achieving certain goals.

For example, in another system, anger management may be a ten-week program where participants learn specific skills in an order, which works well for some people but not for others. Process Work would instead follow the client's feedback at each step, supporting nature in following her message and direction.

Channels of Awareness.

Many approaches to human behavior focus on one or two sensory channels: in contrast, Process Work is a multi-channeled approach. In *The River's Way*, Arnold Mindell states:

> Signals may be differentiated according to the perception sense, which picks them up. Signals and processes are therefore channeled by our senses.... We can therefore visualize, hear, we can feel with our bodies, we can sense movement, we can smell, taste and use combinations of these senses to apprehend signals and processes. (1985, p. 15)

The main sensory channels in process work include the visual channel, or inner and outer seeing, meaning I am either looking at something outside myself or focusing on inner images; the auditory channel, which includes inner and outer listening, meaning listening to sounds in the environment or to sounds inside my head; the proprioceptive channel, which includes feeling body sensations and emotions; and the movement channel, meaning either I experience myself moving my body, my body moving spontaneously, as if it is being moved, or I perceive internal body experiences as moving, i.e., blood rushing through my veins. Smell and taste also emerge as channels, especially with coma patients, although these channels surface less frequently than the others. Therefore, as an aware person around money, one should ask oneself, can I get information from all my channels? Do I notice my visions and dreams? How about the verbal thoughts in my head? How about my body sensations and emotions? What can my movement processes tell me about my money life? How about relationships, can I learn from them about my relationship to money and also how my relationship to money effects my other relationships?

The most commonly used channels also vary from culture to culture. In some Mid-Eastern cultures, smell is more highly utilized to describe experience than it is in the West. In more introverted cultures, people tend to be much more proprioceptive and body aware than people in extraverted cultures. The sensory channels (visual, auditory, proprioception, movement) "couple," that is, combine to form other channels. These include the relationship channel, which includes the relationship between different parts of ourselves, and the relationship between two people or a family, and the world channel, which includes a focus on large groups and social issues. The spiritual channel frequently emerges when working with altered states and spiritual experiences. The relationship, world, and spiritual channels are comprised of several of the basic channels, which include seeing, hearing, feeling, and movement.

Levels of Reality

Like Rabbi Bonder, in *The Kabbalah of Money*, Mindell emphasizes that there are many levels of reality that we need to work with. The levels of reality in Process Work theory include consensus reality, dreamland, and the sentient level. In *Dreaming While Awake*, Mindell defines these levels.

Level one is dreamtime, or sentient reality."Here you notice deep experiences, normally disregarded feelings and sensations that have not yet expressed themselves in terms of meaningful images, sounds, and sensations. These disregarded or marginalized feelings are sentient, that is, preverbal feelings and sensations"(2000, p. 35-36). Only through going deeply into the sentient realm can we attain liberation from the polarities, the lines of either or that have been drawn between wealth and freedom, thus enabling us to have the detachment necessary to know how to follow our true path around issues of money. In the next chapter, we will examine how to apply sentient and dreamwork methods to navigate money.

The next level of reality is dreamland."In dreamland, you notice dreams, fantasies, figures and objects while awake or asleep. You can formulate these experiences more readily in words, in contrast to the experiences of Dreaming, which can barely be grasped in everyday terms." (2000, p. 35). Dreamland will guide us, if we can follow our dreams, through the daily money decisions and directions we have to take. Sentience gives us our central direction in life, and dreamland guides us in how to follow this path.

The final realm of experience he refers to is everyday, or consensus reality."In everyday reality you may use your ordinary attention to notice and share your observations of yourself and others, objects, and ideas. Everyday reality can be described in terms of time and space in contrast to Dreaming and dreamland, whose time and spaces are vastly different from those of everyday reality"(2000, p. 35). Mindell comments, "…the concept of 'reality' is a cultural concept, not an absolute truth.

I have been using the term CR (consensus reality) to refer to the implicit, consensus reality of a given group. In the present book, written with a multicultural population in mind, CR means cosmopolitan reality. This CR marginalizes sentient experiences" (2000, p. 46). Mindell also talks about consensus reality in terms of physics."CR is the world of experimental physics, where you can measure signals and make observations. From the cosmopolitan view, consensus reality seems more objective, NCR (non-consensus reality) more subjective." (2000 p. 37)

Primary and secondary process, and the edge.

In addition to noticing levels of reality, one can look at the structure of a process in terms of primary process, secondary process, and the edge that separates the two. What we identify with, the "I" or "we," is part of the individual's and couple's personality that they identify with. Groups, towns, and countries also have primary processes. Secondary processes are the parts that are "not I," or "not we," that are outside of our normal identity.

Mindell organizes the unconscious layers according to identification and awareness. Full awareness is consciousness. Identifying with something, whether personal or collective, and not identifying with something, are the basis for whether this is primary or secondary material. Both are considered unconscious, but secondary material is further from awareness than primary. Thus it is identification, not whether something is repressed (Freud), or personal / collective (Jung), that determines how far this part of oneself is from awareness. The identification approach is culturally flexible. In some cultures, for example, mythical parts of oneself are very much identified with, while in others, they are part of the deepest collective dreams.

Mindell's categorization of material as primary and secondary has several pioneering aspects. Identification of who we are is signal based, that is, my primary and secondary parts of myself make themselves present in my signals (rather than inferred by the therapist). These signals provide the facilitator a structure to work with in navigating the unconscious.

The therapist hears the clients' description of who they are and can see this in their verbal and non-verbal signals. The therapist can then unfold the secondary process from those signals present that the client doesn't identify with. The therapist finds processes can be denoted in terms of not only signals and sensory channels, but primary and secondary aspects. This approach allows a facilitator to work with previously mysterious territory such as coma states and large group processes, which the map of the conscious and unconscious did not navigate.

People have primary and secondary processes around money. I may identify myself as someone who could care less about money, but I may be constantly dreaming about winning the lottery and other ways of striking it rich. This would come out in my unconscious signals, this interest in money. For example, I have a friend I will call Sam. Sam is always talking about how he doesn't care about money, and yet the always talking about it shows that in some way he does care about it. If every time I meet you I have to tell you how much I don't care about money, it means another part of me is so focused on money that it is all I can talk about. To enter into the world of money consciously, we need awareness of all the parts of ourselves surrounding money.

When I began to do self-destructive trades in the stock market, I had to get in touch with the part of myself that felt I didn't deserve money, as well as the part that was afraid to have money, thinking it would somehow make me less spiritual or something like that. All of my belief systems, conscious and unconscious had to come forward and be examined. Without this necessary step, I would be like a poker player who doesn't even know what cards he has—and still bets.

If someone wants to invest on a regular basis, my own recommendation is that they devote some time to personal growth work, either with themselves, or a professional, on a regular basis. Without, they will not only be having to deal with whatever medium they are working in, such as real estate, the stock market, etc., but they will not know themselves well enough to comprehend which direction they should go at any one point. Accordingly, if I know myself well enough, I know how to find out what Nature is asking of me at any given moment.

The "edge" separates primary and secondary processes. Edges show up in areas of money around knowing oneself, around knowing when to act and when not to act, as well as in believing in oneself. Being stuck on the verge of doing something but not being able to fully do it is being at the edge. At the edge, people create new patterns for going into unknown parts of themselves. We often find symptoms at the edge, which is a place of powerful dreaming and potential energy. We also find *edge figures*, or internal and external figures and people who tell us not to change, not to go into new parts of life and ourselves.

We also find cultural voices. For example, after I had my first counseling job for a while, working in a school as a contracted psychotherapist, I became antsy to move on. My parents advised me to stay—it was the first decent money I had made. They were my edge figures, telling me all the terrible things that might happen if I quit the job, in terms of future work. I did move on, and of course it worked out well or I wouldn't be here writing books today. Whenever I come to a point in my career where I need to move on in some way, these internalized edge figures resurface. Similar edge figures come up with so many of the people I have worked with.

A great place to meet edges is around work issues. I have worked with hundreds of men and women over the years who have come in and told me that they want to quit their jobs. Many have reasons that insist that some change must happen. For example, they are so unhappy with work that they are drinking, or suicidal. They are often at the edge to quit and move into something that would make them much more happy. Yet at the edge comes up all kinds of voices of family and culture.

Recently I worked with a man who hated his job, and was sinking into alcoholism to cope with his unhappiness around his job. I asked him why he didn't change jobs. He had his own catastrophic expectations, that despite a great resume, he would never have a good job again. Also at the edge were all kinds of cultural voices that said that he had to be a good family man and a good provider, and that this was much more important than his happiness.

It was only by becoming aware of these voices that he was able to really study with careful awareness all aspects of his job. He was able to make internal and external changes so that he could keep his job, while finding personal satisfaction and stopping drinking. Yet, without awareness of these forces sticking him and trapping him at the edge, there was no possibility of moving forward. I have experienced personally probably every possible edge around money. I have had edges to have it, to not have it, to pursue money with a passion, and to let go of doing this. Each of us needs to walk our own path and get to know all the different edges we have around money. There are as many different edges around money as there are people. There are edges to make money, to hold on to money, and to let it go. Caring about money can be an edge as well as letting it go and just relaxing and feeling the universe will take care of you.

Exercises

The purpose of this next series of exercises is to help you apply these basic Process Work concepts to your relationship with money.

EXERCISE: Edges and Money

1. If you had one central growing edge around money, what would it be? Here are some possibilities—to make more money; make less money; save more; spend more; enjoy money more; give away more; track your finances and accounts better; make money in the ways you have always dreamed of making money.

2. Pick some edge and talk about or write about what it is like for you to have that edge. Is there an even deeper edge involved?

3. Talk about what it would take to get over that edge. Could you do it with encouragement alone? If not, what psychological and material steps would you need to take to get there?

4. Imagine you are over that edge. How would your life change?

5. Make a plan to take at least a step or two in the direction of this change.

EXERCISE: Primary and Secondary Processes and Money

1. Imagine someone was interviewing you about who you are around money. How would you describe yourself?

2. Now while you are describing this, take notice of a double signal: something your body is doing that doesn't quite go along with what you are describing. For example, if you say you are someone who is relaxed around money and you are squirming in your seat, notice the squirming and focus on it.

3. Amplify the secondary signal, that is do it more, feel it more, let it express itself until you know what it is expressing.

4. Take some time to do this until you feel something shift. Now try to integrate the two parts of yourself, the primary identity and what you discovered in the double signal. Make a verbal description that somehow includes both of these parts of yourself.

5. Take some time to feel and get to know who you would be if you had access and could get to know both of these parts of your money related self.

EXERCISE: Money and the Evolving Self

1. Create a timeline around money. Start by drawing a line long enough you can put several different time slots on this line. Leave space under the line to write comments.

2. Start to mark significant places on your time line. For example, this is me as a child with money, here is me at age, and so on. Continue up to the present day, and then make two additional slots, one for the near future and one for the distant future.

3. Now make small comments under the time slots, or draw small pictures. Here is little Suzy at five and she thinks money is really fun. Here she is at nine earning her money helping mom or dad do this or that. Make a few slots that go beyond the current time section of your chart and allow yourself to imagine into the next steps coming.

4. Take time to study the flow of events and notice what trends are present and which aren't. Write down three statements that present general themes of growing and learning present in your relationship to money. How are these themes present in other parts of your life in addition to your financial life?

5. What potential areas of growth around your money related path does your timeline suggest? Name the three next steps in your evolvement.

Social Issues and Process Work

Process Work also places significance on examining problems in social and political contexts. Individual psychological and body experiences, relationship problems, and world conflicts all have elements of collective issues and change. We need not only to bring the world into our individual, couple, and family sessions by representing world issues such as sexism, racism, and homophobia; we also need a method to work with these social issues in groups. Worldwork developed out of a sociopolitical perspective on problems, with aims to fill in a missing gap in therapies and provide a way of working with problems in a group setting.

With this strong emphasis on taking social issues into account, we cannot look at money issues from only the standpoint of personal psychology—or even that of mysticism—without also being willing to look at the social issues involved in a world where so few have so much, and so many so little. We cannot clearly comprehend individual fate around money without taking into consideration how society has stacked the deck, making it easy for some to have, and near impossible for others. While it is dangerous to the individual to operate in the money world without knowledge of who they are psychologically and spiritually, and how these worlds affect their approach to money, it is equally dangerous for us to act as if money is played on a level field. This unconsciousness could encourage one to stop making the efforts that are so vital in bringing more of a sense of justice and equality to the great disparities that exist in the world between rich and poor people, and rich and poor nations.

We understand from the mystical texts we have already reviewed, and from Process Work, that there are many kinds of wealth, and that many poor people may be much wealthier in terms of spiritual wealth than financially rich people—yet the area of financial well-being is also important. On the other end, to ignore spiritual power often causes one to be condescending toward people who have grown up with less. The whole issue of money is a political discussion; bringing more awareness to this area isn't simply about helping people to better navigate the waters of personal economics, it is also a political act.

Money is political. Awareness of money means not only that of my own dreaming process around it, but awareness of the great inequalities that exist worldwide and what each individual can do to help with this global situation. I am presenting some facts about global poverty here so that we can all be aware of how much inequality there is. My goal isn't to make those of us who have more feel guilty, but to celebrate the incredible privilege we have, and become inspired to use it to benefit others. Here are some difficult and alarming facts from the website.

- Half of the world's population, over 3 billion people, live on less than $2 per day.

- In 2000, 1.7 million children died in the world due to poverty related causes.

- A few hundred millionaires in the world own as much as the world's 2.5 billion poorest people.

- The two hundred richest people in the world had net worth over 1 trillion dollars in 1999, and the combined worth of 582 million people in 43 of the least developed countries was 146 billion dollars.

I could continue on with facts like this, but the point is not to depress us or condemn those who have, nor to make the rest of the world appear to be victims. The purpose is to exposethe disparity that exists and continues to grow. Here in the United States, "Occupy Wall Street," the original that began the worldwide beginning September 17, 2011, developed, with their emphasis in bringing public awareness to the reality of the wealthy 1% owning more than the 99% of the rest of the population.

As a Process Worker, I am committed to helping those with economic privilege gain awareness of these disparities, and to address them accordingly. For one person this might mean having less and giving away more to help others. For another person, this might motivate them to make even more money so as to be able to help others, and for others, it may be their process to just take a minute and be aware of the suffering involved in this area of world wealth and poverty.

Meditating on human suffering can light a fire in many people to do something about the world and its problems.

This brings to mind the Gates family and all their wealth from Microsoft, who in the last few years have created a charitable foundation that is addressing many of the world's most serious problems. Yes this is generous, and it is a privilege as well to have so much to give others, however each of us is a bit like the Gates family. We each have something to contribute to make the world less of a place of suffering. I think of one of my friends, who at Christmas time goes to the local mall and pulls tags off a tree to buy presents for many families in need. Little things like this, if we all did them, would make a huge difference.

We are asked to give to so many causes, as there are endless hurricanes, tsunamis, famines and wars. Even so, we have so much to give. The more we are connected with the world's issues, the richer we are, experiencing more of ourselves as a greater part of a global community. The more we become aware of all aspects of money, the more compassion we can develop for ourselves and for all beings that somehow depend on money to live.

This is fundamental to Process Work theory. We don't try to deny or eliminate the sources of our rank, but instead use our awareness to share this rank with others. Part of sharing our rank is stepping out of our own comfort zones and intentionally being aware of the economic suffering of the world. The next step is to do something about this disparity. This might include the personal donation of time or money, and also pressing the government of our cities, states, and nations to face issues of economic disparity and economic injustice This also includes opening our eyes to the fact that much of so-called terrorism and violence is not behavior inherent in who those involved truly are, but is often actually an act of desperation. Much of this desperation is economically based. I have been very touched, for example, through my work in the Middle East with Palestinians and Israelis.

There are many Israeli businessmen and businesswomen who are committed to making change through opening businesses that can directly have a positive impact on the Palestinian community. Good economic practice is part of peace making. In continuing to raise economic awareness around socio-political issues, it is important to see that although we could rant and rave about drug wars in Central and South America, and even our own cities, we need to also be awake to the economics of drugs. If the only way to make a living for many people these parts of the world is in raising poppy or trafficking drugs, no matter how many of the "bad guys" we can get our hands on in jail, we won't make any real change; not until it pays as much to grow beans as it does the poppy that can be made into opium. In the next chapter I will go into detail about issues of rank and power and how to work with these from a Process Work perspective.

EXERCISE: Positive Use of Your Economic Rank
Here is a brief exercise with the purpose of focusing on giving with awareness, using your economic rank to help others.

1. Think of someone who financially has less than you, and who you care about deeply.

2. Think of one act you could make to help this person that they would feel good about receiving.

3. Act upon this.

4. Now think of one world project that you know needs help.

5. Do something, even if it is small, to contribute to this world project.

6. Notice how this may be changing your feelings about yourself and/or the world.

Process Work Tools for Working with Money

Process Work addresses a wide variety of personal and societal concerns, including body symptoms, relationship problems, addictions, extreme psychological states, coma and head injury, inner work, group work and world conflict work. There are four main parts of Process Work that we need to be familiar with in order to work effectively on issues around finance.

Firstly, we need to know about working with our dreams, whereas this will be one of the areas we use to guide us. We will need to know how to access the sentient level, this deepest feeling, non-dualistic level; we need to know our deepest callings, our life path, and to have healthy detachment necessary to work on difficult money issues.

Furthermore, addictions and addictive tendencies play a tremendous role in the subject of money; we need to know how to work with our addictions, to both having and not having money. Finally, we need to be able to know how to maintain awareness and engage personally with

Worldworkand global issues, thus enabling us to put money issues into the proper context.

I could, and in fact have, written entire books on each of these four areas. In this book, however, my purpose is to give the reader enough of a taste of each of these areas to inspire and empower them to practice, understand, and apply the methods for their own benefit.

Dreams In General

Let us begin by working with dreams. There are so many ways to interpret and work with dreams to achieve greater understanding. The three levels important in being able to work with on dreams around money are 1 to work with the literal level of the dream, that is following its guidance as if it were part of waking reality, 2 to work with the symbolic level, to interpret dreams to get their meaning, and 3 to work with the sentient level, going under the dream, deeper and beyond what the dream offers, therefore contacting the original energy the dream brings.

The sentient level is closest to those moments of clarity we experience at times when we wake up with the middle of the night. Sentience focuses more on the Source of dreams, the Dreammaker, rather than the dreams themselves. Here are examples of each level, and how to work with each level. Some dreams give information which is meant to be taken literally. If you dream your refrigerator is broken, it may be that part of you has been noticing unusual noises from the refrigerator, and not paying attention to it. Perhaps it really is broken.

Some of these dreams are prophetic—they foretell the future. There are many debates about how these precognitive, predictive dreams occur. One of the most common answers to this phenomenon, is that we dream about what we already perceive, coming in small and subtle signals, such as the refrigerator breaking slowly in little ways we would not pay much attention to.

The other major explanation of this occurrence is that dreams are somehow non-local, that is to say, they put us into a realm that doesn't follow consensus reality's rules of time and space. Here and there are no longer separated, they simply appear to be. Many people for example, tell me that they had dreamt of a relative who died, right before they in fact did die. In my last class on relationships, I asked how many people had the experience of dreaming of someone they met before they had actually met and entered a major relationship with the person, and several had.

A major factor in having such experiences is that of how much we pay attention to our dreams. For example, I have always dreamt of a new partner right before I meet someone new to start a long-term relationship. I could always tell when it was coming. Some money dreams are very literal. In my experience, the more I opened up to looking at my dreams around the stock market, the more I could connect with this flow, where my dreams would accurately tell me whether the market was going to go up and down, and sometimes by exact numbers.

As I mentioned earlier in the book, when I had a dream that the markets were going to go through big losses, right around the time of the Dot.com Crash, I called my father. I said, "Dad, most of your investments are in stock. You have done well. Get out of most of it. I have had several dreams that the market is going to crash." He was very sweet, but said he had enormous amounts of faith in the United States economy, and that he saw the markets only growing. A few months later the markets crashed, and he lost big time.

Most dreams have a literal level, but are primarily in code, in imagery and other symbols that we need to be able to interpret. I have been teaching dreamwork classes for 33 years. People always ask me how to distinguish between a dream that is symbolic, and one that is literal. This comes out of experience. I can feel the difference, and often hear it when someone tells a dream. All dreams have some kind of literal level, but those that are primarily meant to be interpreted literally carry a certain kind of matter-of-fact crispness to them.

Knowing how to interpret dreams is something that needs to be practiced. Many of us have natural gifts as dreamers and dream interpreters, and yet we still can benefit from practicing. Each person's experience is different, but for myself, to reach a state where I can get almost daily information from my dreams about the stock market takes a certain manner of daily communion with my dreams. It means I look toward them, work with them, and follow them. When I stopped paying regular attention to my dreams, I lost the ability to follow the market in my dreams; it was only after returning to intentional awareness and respect for my dreams that I finally got this back. If in dreams we leave ordinary time and space, then it is feasible that we will be able to know what is happening before it happens. Once more, this is an art to be cultivated with intentional awareness and consistency. My awareness of my Tuesday night dreams begins on Monday. I can notice what little sensations and feelings I put aside during my busy day and my consciousness that tends to marginalize certain thoughts and feelings. My dreamer is like a dream catcher that catches all of these fragments I push aside and uses them at night to paint a collage—to give me visual pictures of all these cast aside parts. I should be able to predict what I will dream if I just catch a glimpse of what I cast aside.

The second level of dreamwork is to work with the symbols of the dream. There are several effective ways in which to approach this work. I always begin working with other's dreams by asking them to associate with the dream symbol. If someone dreams of a seal, I ask them to associate with a seal, finding what this feels like and means to them. This is very different from the literal realm. Stating that a seal is a type of animal that eats this and does that, is describing the consensus reality information about the animal. Associations show what that seal means to oneself. One of the best ways to find these associations is to simply chat with someone, or write about the symbol. Chatting might look something like asking the person if they like seals, what they feel when they see or read about one, and what comes into their mind when they think of seals.

Another way to reveal associations is through getting what Dr. Arnold Mindell refers to as "pop-up associations." This process simply involves asking the person what pops up into their mind when they think of seals. Putting together the different associations to the dream symbols then leads to an interpretation. There are many ways to move on from here. Gestalt therapy and Process Work help us to step into the dream and play out the figures. This gives us more access to the energy of the dream figures as well as their symbolic meaning. Process Work helps us follow the dream in whatever channels of perceiving we receive the dream in. A dream that is full of visual scenes suggests visual ways of working further.

In working to better understand my dream, I might focus on one symbol and meditate on it, or picture the dream continuing further on, a process referred to as "dreaming the dream onward," or I might imagine what came before the dream. The Jungians especially deserve credit for all the ways of working with active imagination and visualization. I might also paint the dream. If it is a dream full of movement, I might get up and move with the dream, finding its meaning through dance. A dream full of sound might lead me to making noises or singing parts or the whole story of the dream. Some dreams are full of feelings, and I might go into my body and feel and amplify the feelings I am having.

If a dream is based on relationship, I myself could play out the different roles and have them interact, taking the other person as parts of myself, or perhaps have a friend do this kind of relationship role-playing with me. I may tell the dream to the person in the dream and see how they react. The person's reaction is also part of my feedback for dream interpretation. The dream figure of this person may just represent a part of me; may be part of a relationship process with the other person, or both. If I am dreaming about world events, I might take action and do some kind of social action on the topic of the dream, or call a town meeting or a small group to get together and work on this issue. Dreams that seem to carry enormous meaning, spiritual symbols and energy might lead me to create a ritual through which to work with the dream energy, or it may suggest major shifts in how I live my life.

Another way to work with dreams from a Process-Oriented perspective is to ask ourselves about edges. We dream at the edge. I am regularly just about to do or say or feel or think or act or be in certain ways that I marginalize throughout the day, and these edges end up in my dreams. I can work on the dream by asking myself what edge did I get to, which the dream is reflecting for me, and I can work directly on that edge. For example, let's say I have a money mess somewhere in my life that I don't want to look at. I then dream of a horrible mess that disgusts me. With enough awareness, this takes me back to the edge of cleaning up my money mess.

We can also look within the dream itself for the edge the dream is bringing up. If dreams themselves are about our edges, then the edge of the dream, the point in the dream where I reach my limitations somehow, reveals the most difficult part of the edge. Let us imagine that in the dream I am just about to clean up this huge mess in the room, but I have to move something very heavy, and I back off, deciding that I am too weak to move these heavy things. I give up, and the dream shifts. Thus I might focus my edge work right here at this edge, of how I don't feel strong enough somehow to go forward and do what I need to do; I would then work on this edge to my strength.

Next I will describe one of the biggest dreams I have had about money, and the edges it reflected. My full story comes in the next chapter, but to illustrate my point I will share a portion of it. About September, of 2005, I had to get out of the markets. I had decided to put the money into something safer, and also I didn't need all of that stress and time commitment it required.

In addition to working a more than full-time therapy practice, I was doing four hours a day of day trading. The day I was going to pull myself out of the market, my old reliable stock suddenly took a terrible hit, and I lost almost half of what I had made. I was devastated. I had only a few months to try and recover, as I had bought my share of a house on the Oregon coast with the money, and felt I couldn't let others and myself down around this dream. I didn't have enough to cover my share.

I began to work furiously to get the money back, and very slowly I made it back. The markets were in horrible shape, it was the time of hurricane Katrina, and that national tragedy depressed the markets. I saw no way out. I was trapped with not enough time to recover. I would have to surrender to losing the money this time, and instead come up with whatever I could for the house. Instead of taking this relaxed exit, I felt defeated, depressed, and stressed out.

Then abruptly, about a week before I had to get out, the markets began to climb. They made a considerable recovery, which took me to a position where I could get out and my losses would be a third instead of a half of what I had made. I went into a dilemma—how far should I recover, knowing at any moment the markets could retreat from this relief rally?

I went camping, and that night had a dream. I dreamt that there were two ships out on the ocean, and the seas became very rough. There was a big ship and a little ship. The little ship didn't know where to go, but just followed the big ship. Suddenly the little ship saw this sign for a safe harbor, with a specific number on it, and made a sudden turn into the harbor, unsure if it would be safe or not. It turned out that the ship had found a smooth bay to land in. I remembered the number of the harbor. The next morning I awoke feeling a rush of hope. I thought to myself, "Somehow I am going to be all right and get out of this horrible mess." I told myself that if my portfolio reached the value of that number, I would quit on that very day.

A week later, my main stock had an amazing one-day run. It went up so high that I hit my number to get out. At that number, my losses from the original day I had meant to sell would be minimal, about 10%. It was a miracle. I was at a seminar, and the computer line hooking me up the market kept crashing. Suddenly it hit my target, and I began selling. I went into a whirl and sold almost everything I had.

Suddenly I panicked and asked myself if I shouldn't go back in the market, just for the day, long enough to make up the rest of my losses and leave in peace. I went back to the seminar where I saw my long time teacher and mentor, Dr. Arnold Mindell. I told him the dream, that I had sold out, but I thought I should go back in for just a day in this one stock and make up the rest of the loss. He said, "No, your dream was right, let it be."

Today I sit in my coast house, my share paid for, writing this book. The day after this miracle, the markets started plunging again. I wouldn't have had enough for the house. If I would have stayed in for three or four more months, now looking back, I probably would have made lots more money, or not, depending on how I timed things. Despite this, the lesson here is to follow the dreams, not the dollar amount. This dream illustrated two different levels. First, I worked with it symbolically. I had said to myself many times I that I had felt like someone trying to land a plane, or steer a ship to safety in rough conditions.

The dream was about my edge to get out. It showed me how to do it. The edge in the dream was when the little ship turned into the unknown, following intuition, taking a risk, and succeeding in knowing when enough was enough and when it was time to pull into the harbor, to pull in my efforts and energy. The dream was both full of symbolic material (steering the ship to safety), feeling material (giving me hope at the edge), and literal material (a numeric figure to get out at).

The depth of experience and understanding this teaching gave me is at the very core of Process Work: whatever you are dealing with, following the process is what is most important. Far beyond the importance of having a goal of making money, helping someone find healing, etc., In Process Work, the deepest value and belief is in following and trusting nature. Often, when we have a body symptom or a relationship crisis or any big decision around our financial life, we feel as a victim of what is happening. When we look back with some distance from the situation, it is easier to see the meaning and beauty of what we have experienced.

When summer came later on that year I had sold out of the markets, I finally experienced reaching a place of significant clarity and peace of mind. It happened after a day of cycling, writing, running, and spending time with family. I found myself riding my bike along the coast, coming to a clear understanding of the wisdom of the path I had followed. At first after leaving the market, when I saw one of the stocks I had sold had soared up many dollars within a few weeks, I experienced pangs of regret for what I could have made. However, with the insight and wisdom gained from several months of perspective, I came to a place of never looking back. What the dream had shown me was right, I needed a safe harbor. The process of playing the markets was right for me until that very moment the dream revealed, then it was time to exit. Dreams help us counter our tendency to be stuck in one role or pole. Stay in, get out. Invest. Run. If we work on them, our dreams help keep us fluid, enabling us to move with the changing tides.

Another key focus at the level of dreams is that our dreams are full of roles. These roles are the same as the characters actors play in the script of a play or movie. At the level of dreams, there are still hierarchies of higher and lower, and issues of rank and power. Here I quote from my book,

Beyond War and Peace in the Arab Israeli Conflict, where I define what rank and power issues are:

> One of the other issues that is important in resolving the conflict is to address rank directly. Rank is made up of all powers and privileges, earned or unearned, that a person carries with them. There are many sources of rank and power, including economic, social rank, race, class, gender, sexual identity, spiritual centeredness, psychological well-being, health, nationality, and other sources. Social rank has to do with the status you have based on mainstream culture. Society assigns this rank based on race, sexual orientation, health, class, age, and gender. Structural rank comes from the power assigned to positions that come from the hierarchies within institutions, as well as the career paths, which carry more rank than others. Psychological rank has to do with how comfortable one is with themselves, their relationships, and other parts of their life. This comes from our childhood experiences as well as our later life experiences. Spiritual rank has to do with the centeredness that comes from feeling very closely connected to your spiritual source or center. Often oppressed groups develop spiritual rank, partially out of their suffering.
>
> Rank that is unconscious continues to inflame and keep the polarities growing. World Work brings a specific philosophy to this work. Many people think they should hide their rank in a group situation in order to not inflame the other side, but this seems to inflame the situation even more. The method we encourage is to state one's rank con-

sciously, and to then utilize these advantages for the benefit of others. (2004, p.43)

Why is it so important to think about rank when we work on dreams? For the reason that our dreams are partially organized by the various social issues and pressures we live under. Remember how Rabbi Bonder said over and over again that making money is holy, yet it must be tied to the wellness of all beings? I am not just to enhance my own stash of money, but to do something for humanity along with, and also through this.

Without awareness of issues of rank, any of us could easily get lost in our own gain without concern for others. In fact, many say that this is one of the major problems with modern society and even modern religion—that there is not enough concern for the needy and less fortunate. Without awareness of rank and how different kinds of rank each carry varying kinds of power, we may begin to look down on and patronize those who have less social or economic rank then ourselves.

I remember being in India in the ocean one day and a very kind man began to talk with me. He essentially told me that I probably have much more money then he does, but he doesn't work so hard. He enjoys his life. For a period of time, he had left to another country to make some money and save it, and now at a fairly young age he was able to take it easy. The man had finally opened a little neighborhood store because at times he enjoyed working in such a manner. The rest of the time he was with his children and family relaxing.

Who was the wealthier? He seemed to feel sorry for me. At first I was most perplexed by this. I don't want to minimize the poverty and suffering in India; although this man wasn't poor or suffering, there are innumerable Indians living in poverty and as beggars. I received great lessons from some of the beggars I was also fortunate enough to interact with. Through all of this, I couldn't understand how some of them seemed so happy and in such bliss? It shocked me and woke me up to matter of spiritual rank and the understanding that happiness is not so tied to money as we in the West so often think.

However, having said this, each group needs to use their rank for the benefit of all. If I am someone poor who has developed tremendous inner powers from my suffering, I can share these teachings and this power with others. If I have money, and/or know how to make money, I can share this rank with those who do not. I never had much money as an adult, and now at the age of fifty-eight I am finally doing pretty well in this area. Consequently, I am in part writing this book to use my rank to help spread whatever good fortune I have received to those who may benefit from it.

Dreams and Money

One of the central points of this book is that money is not simply money alone, but it is deeply connected with feelings, relationships, spirituality, and world issues. All of the methods presented so far in this book are to help you to go deeper into your connections with and understanding of money. In the following chapter, written on my personal life, I share how my dreams play the role of my guide, both my night dreams and my daytime dreamlike experiences. In this next chapter, we will look at both how to work with dreams in general, and specifically, dreams of money.

Our daily experiences of money are not only part of the material and everyday reality. When the national lottery gets up to several hundred million dollars, I am amazed at how many clients come in telling me they have either dreamt or fantasized about what they will do with that money if they win. I have heard interviews with former winners of some of the bigger lotteries. The reality of having the money often is not as fun as the fantasy. At least one major winner, when interviewed, said he wished he had never won because of all of the family and relationship troubles that it caused. Even so, dreaming we are wealthy is a powerful theme, and I will talk later in chapter 3 about the specific meaning of such dreams.

Let's start at square one by reviewing some of the methods of dreamwork I mentioned earlier in this chapter, and go deeper into these methods of dreamwork applied to dreamwork with money dreams. Many people would like to know more about their dreams, yet don't remember them, much less understand what they mean. I have taught dream classes in some form or another for over thirty years. I aim to glean some of the basic lessons from those classes, and then add on what I have learned from my clients, my own dreams, and my studies in Process-oriented Psychology.

Firstly, dreams are like any other parts of our bodies and personalities in that they thrive with positive attention and care. Making an effort to remember your dreams, and somehow writing or recording them and sharing them with others seem to strengthen a person's recollections. Many indigenous cultures were aware of this, for example the Huichol in Mexico would have the community gather and tell their dreams to a fire built for this very purpose. One of the main obstacles with remembering dreams is that unless we are experienced with this, dream recall disappears very quickly upon awakening.

However, if we simply write down a few key words as we are waking, or speak them into a recorder, we will often have captured enough to advance the next step. It is both the physical act of writing, and that we are setting our intent on remembering, that has a positive effect. What also helps is to lie in bed a few minutes after waking with your eyes closed, feeling the moods or state that you have awoke with. This often leads to having dreams come back into memory. Sharing your dreams with someone also helps strengthen this intent to remember, and is actually a way of working on dreams. Many times people will suddenly have an insight into the meaning of a dream through sharing it alone. In terms of working with dreams, there are so many different methods, it would take a book in itself to go into all of them in depth. In what follows, however, I'll take some time to describe the basics of the different methods:

To begin, all methods somehow work with amplifying and highlighting different aspects of the dreams. Some are more analytic, some experiential. Process-oriented Psychology is both analytic and experiential. I often start with my clients by using basic Jungian-style interventions, and move on from there. I will ask the client to tell the dream, and then to associate with different dream symbols. There are two kinds of associations.

The first is a more reflective association. If someone dreams of a horse, there association with that might be something like freedom, power, etc.. This association is much more than a description, such as an animal used for farming, transportation, and recreation. The second kind of association is what Dr. Arnold Mindell calls a "pop-up" association. This would be the first thing that pops into your mind when you say the word horse. For myself at the moment, I think of wild oneness; when I ride the horse the feeling is incredibly wild, while feeling strongly connected to myself and to the horse. The pop up association is more spontaneous and possibly closer to the essence of the symbol. Robert Johnson, a famous Jungian analyst, talked about the importance of being able to add up all of these different symbols meanings into one statement that summarized the meaning of the dream. This is similar to Mindell's method of walking vectors to get to the meaning of a dream, but that comes a bit later in this chapter.

For now, let's go further into Jungian methods. We can work visually with the dream in what the Jungians call active imagination. This means we can visually work with the dream through either re-imagining the dream, or working with some kind of art medium, for example, clay sculpting, painting, or drawing. When working visually, I use three main methods. The first I call working forwards, or imagining that the dream hadn't stopped where it did, but continued further on. The second I call working backwards, or imagining what happened that led up to the dream, visualizing the equivalent to the previous chapter in the dream.

Finally, I do what I call working sideways, which is to go further into working with one symbol, and see how that symbol transforms through focusing on it in my imagination or in my clients' imaginations. In addition to exploring the more personal unconscious aspects of the symbol, Jungians also study the archetypal, universal meaning behind symbols in order to delve deeper into their meaning in terms of the collective unconscious.

For example, someone dreams that they win the lottery and are trying to figure out what to do with all of that money. I might have them continue further in this dream, and perhaps what would come up is what they would do with all this money, or the celebration, and so on. Then we might progress backward in the dream and see what comes beforehand which makes this dream so meaningful and puts it in a context. Or I might help them to associate with the different elements of the dream, such as a person buying a ticket, the little store they buy it at, the clerk at the store, the lottery ticket and the lottery itself. We would work on the interpretation of the dream through the client's associations, or I might talk with them about the symbols of gambling and winning and the meaning of these symbols in general, as well as the levels of risk taking and reward, and what interpretations may go along with this.

Let us now look into more experiential methods. When I was a Gestalt therapist, I learned three main tools that I still use today. The main approach is become the different symbols in the dream. In our example of the horse, I am not only looking into the meaning of the horse, but I actually become the horse. The second principle, after focusing on becoming the horse, is to go deeper into letting its energy come through, creating more than an intellectual understanding of the dream, but a felt embodied experience. A next step would be to let the various different symbols interact. Perhaps there is a horse and a horse rider, and I go back and forth being each of them and letting the two interact. The third main principle that I still use is to go for the heat of the dream, where the energy is, and focus my work there. For instance, someone dreams that they are diving down into an old ship, and find a treasure chest in the ship that they can't get open. In the Gestalt method, I might have them take turns becoming the diver, the ship, and the treasure chest and explore that experience. I would then have them go back and forth between the diver and the treasure chest that won't open up, until the meaning of all this becomes clear.

Process-oriented Psychology is the primary method I utilize, which has many central principles around dreams. For further detail, I would recommend reading Dr. Arnold

Mindell's books, especially *Dreambody, The Dreamaker's Apprentice,* and *Dreaming While Awake*. From this approach, the first principle I use is that the dream is both in the dream world and in the body. Therefore I can also work on the dream by having people locate the symbol in their bodies. Through this principal, I can do similar work to that of the two roles dialoguing in the Gestalt approach; I can have someone place their hands at different points on their body where they feel the symbols, and then have the symbols connect together on some kind of energetic level. It is hard to explain, but comes clear if you try it. First remember a dream, then feel where in your body each symbol is located. Next, place one hand on one of these locations, and your other hand on the other. Imagine that the two are energetically connected, and then notice what happens.

We can also access dreams through the body. Often times when people are working on a body symptom in a Process-oriented way, if they go deep enough into this symptom work, they will suddenly remember a dream. Accordingly, we can go from dream to body and body to dream. Take for example, I have a dream that I lost my wallet full of money, and someone finds it and gives it to me, but the money however, is gone. In working with this dream, I might feel where I notice the wallet in my body, then where the person who finds it is located, and have those two body locations communicate with each other with energy and words.

The second main Process Work principle I utilize around dreams is working with the channels of awareness through which the dream occurs, as mentioned earlier in the chapter. A dream with many visual symbols I would work with visually; dreams with lots of sound or music I would work with through audition and sound; a dream full of movement would be great to work with movement approaches; a dream with lots of relationship issues would be appropriate to work with role playing and relationships; lastly, a dream full of feeling might be best worked with by having the person focus on emotions and body sensations. Thereupon, returning to the dream earlier about swimming in the ocean to a buried ship and trying to open the treasure chest, I might work with movement, having the person swim and then try and pry open the chest, working with what comes up from there.

The third principle is that when someone tells a dream, it is somehow happening in the moment. If I tell the dream about opening the treasure chest, while I am telling it there must be someway that I am swimming, possibly in the roundabout way I tell the dream; there must be a way that I can't quite get something to open up, whether it is within myself, or between myself and who I am telling the dream to. I would therefore bring this idea up with the client and investigate deeper into it. I might say to them, "I see how you are struggling right now with how to open up more, and have more access to those feelings. They are your real treasure; let's open that chest up and let some of them out. How can we help you to open up right now?"

The fourth principle I use through Process Work is that people dream right at the edges in their development. The dream is a picture of where the person is stuck and trying to grow past their limitations. For example, I have a friend who is a therapist and is trying to expand what they do beyond private practice, into teaching and worldwork through some form of social action. She is always dreaming about working with large groups. Before I started working with large group conflicts, in my practice, I dreamt that I was teaching at a football stadium full of people. The dream was showing me that I was working on opening up to the world more. With our dreams, we can work on the dream content, or simply focus on the edge that is trying to develop. I might say to the therapist, that I appreciate the way the dream points out how she is working on expanding her work, and I would like to focus on what keeps her from expanding her ability to reach more people, create more change in the world, and also potentially make more money.

The fifth principle is that we can reach the dreaming realms anytime, not only when asleep. This is why Mindell calls his book *Dreaming While Awake*, techniques for 24 hour lucid dreaming. Mindell defines the difference between what he calls dreamtime, or sentient reality, and dreamland. He says of dreamtime, "Here you notice deep experiences, normally disregarded feelings and sensations that have not yet expressed themselves in terms of meaningful images, sounds, and sensations. These disregarded or marginalized feelings are sentient, that is, preverbal feelings and sensations. (2000, p. 34-35). In terms of dreamland, he says, "In Dreamland, you notice dreams, fantasies, figures, and objects while awake or asleep. You can formulate these experiences more readily in words, in contrast to the experiences of Dreaming, which can barely be grasped in everyday terms."(2000, p.35) Lucid dreaming refers to awareness of all levels, these two dream levels, and everyday, consensus reality. He defines lucidity as "awareness of the dream's entire pre-meaning sense, which, when unfolded, leads to the meaning of the parts of the dream. Consciousness values the parts and seeks meaning and interconnection between them but easily ignores the awesomeness of the Dreaming that is prior to the concept of meaning."(2000, p. 62) He continues, saying that those moments when you are both lucid and conscious can be called at least momentarily, enlightenment.

The central question to ask from the sentient standpoint is, "What is nature unfolding here?," "What is trying to happen, and what is the meaning from the perspective of nature's eyes?" Considering sentience is pre-verbal, it is most important to express this realm through creative expression that goes beyond the linear use of words. These other modes of expression include dance and other forms of movement, song, drama, poetry, painting, sculpture, and other forms of artistic expression. There are many ways to access this realm that we will be discussing momentarily.

One of the most frequent questions that comes up while working with people is, "How do I know if I am in the sentient realm?" There are many different ways to experience this. There is a notable depth of experience, a sense of oneness with oneself and the experience. There is often a feeling of being bigger than your ordinary self, in terms of energy, perspective, and dimension of experience. One of the real keys is that as people drop down in the different worlds to sentience, they often still experience parts of themselves against having that experience. In Process Work terms, we would say they come up against edges and edge figures. However, in the sentient realm, there is no opposition to the experience or its expression. The more we are in touch with the sentient realm, the more mediumistic we become. You can be in relationship and feel what is present in the atmosphere. You can know what is coming in relationship by catching the littlest flirts, the most interesting pieces of awareness normally ignored.

Stepping into this kind of 24 hour dreaming involves several different methods. First, I can catch flickers or flirts, those "nano-awareness" moments when something just touches my awareness and I then chose to go deeper into it. I am including here an excerpt from my book on Coma Work, Inside Coma, written with Dr. Pierre Morin, to help show how to get used to working in these sentient realms so that we can apply these tools to our money work. To begin, let's look at a basic exercise, which enables us drop into sentient realms.

All of the following exercises in this chapter are based on the work of Dr. Arnold and Dr. Amy Mindell, and I apply these methods specifically to issues of money.

The only way to truly understand the applications of Process Work to money issues is to experience this oneself. This is why we are now going into a whole series of exercises, as with the experiential part of this learning you will be able to integrate these teachings into your body and your dreams.

EXERCISE: Working with Flirts

The purpose of this exercise is to learn how to work with the flirts that grab our attention as a gateway into the essence level.

1. Sit quietly and take a few breaths.

2. Close your eyes and let your mind become cloudy and unknowing. When your mind is empty, slowly open your eyes and notice whatever first catches your attention.

3. Shape-shift into the thing that caught your attention. For example, if you saw a picture of a river on the wall, become the river.

4. Now imagine that you could look back at yourself through the eyes of the river (or whatever caught your attention.). What does the river see when it looks at you?

5. Next, see if you can look at yourself and the river from the perspective of the Big You, which sees both the river

and you as part of the same whole. Take this as a momentary picture of the deeper you that is trying to be present.

6. Imagine that you are this whole self. Is there any way in which having access to your whole self might help with your struggles in some area of your life?

When I want to move into the sentient realm, I use my eyes, hands, general awareness, and my energy differently. Here are some exercises to help you further in getting in touch with how to be in contact with and work with the sentient level of awareness.

Applying Flirt Work

The purpose of this inner work is to practice catching flirts as a way of working on a specific problem, in this case a body symptom.

1. Take an inner scan of your body.

2. Catch a body feeling that catches your attention, perhaps one that is surprising (something more subtle and small, not too overwhelming).

3. Place your focus there. Feel it and try to amplify a bit. It sometimes helps to breathe into that spot.

4. Try to get to the essence. First the tendency, then the seed, before it got so big and became a larger feeling in body. Let your mind formulate this and use it as you like. Express this essence through movement and sound, until you can name the un-named.

5. What can you learn from this essence for yourself. Where do you need more of this essential quality in your inner and or outer life at this time?

EXERCISE: Applying Working with Flirts to Money Issues

The purpose of this exercise is to apply techniques of working with flirts specifically to issues around money.

1. First think of a money problem you struggle with. Then put it aside, sit quietly and take a few breaths.

2. Close your eyes and let your mind become cloudy and unknowing. When your mind is empty, slowly open your eyes and notice whatever first catches your attention.

3. Shape-shift into the thing that caught your attention. For example, if you saw a picture of a river on the wall, become the river.

4. Now imagine that you could look back at yourself through the eyes of the river (or whatever caught your attention.). What does the river see when it looks at you?

5. Next, see if you can look at yourself and the river from the perspective of the Big You, which sees both the river and you as part of the same whole. Take this as a momentary picture of the deeper you that is trying to be present.

6. Imagine that you are this whole self. Is there any way in which having access to your whole self might help with your struggles in some area of your life?

7. How was this experience somehow an answer to your money problem you raised in step 1?

EXERCISE: Sentient Work on Body Experiences Connected with Money

The purpose of this exercise is to give you a body based method of working at the essence level regarding your relationship to money.

1. Think of a money issue or problem you have. Now set it aside. Take an inner scan of your body—start up at your head and work down to your toes, noticing what asks for or draws your attention.

2. Take note of a body feeling that catches your attention, perhaps that is surprising (something more subtle and small, not too overwhelming).

3. Place your focus there. Feel it and try to amplify a bit. Sometimes it helps to breathe into that spot.

4. Try to get to the essence, the first tendency, the seed, before it got so big and became a larger feeling in your body. For example, if you have a pounding headache, the essence of that pounding might be something like the sound of a gong, waking you up, therefore being awake might be the essence. Let your mind formulate this and use it as you like. Express this essence through movement and sound, until you can name the un-named. Along with the example, if this essence were being awake, I would show awakened state, or awakening, through movement and sound.

5. What can you learn from this essence for yourself.

6. Think of a way to bring this learning back into your daily life, and of specifically how is this essence awareness an answer to your money issue.

Now how do these apply to the world of money? Either of these methods can take you to your essence when you need to be there. In my worst moments, I go back to these kinds of basic exercises. They also help us to access what Mindell calls 24-hour dreaming. This means I don't have to fall asleep in order to access the deep dreaming part of myself. I simply close my eyes for a moment, and catch a flicker of awareness and unfold that flicker. For those who aren't as visual or proprioceptive, able to access information from the body feelings, there are movement-based approaches. Here is the most common movement access use:

1. Focus on an issue you have around money. State the issue.

2. Now simply begin moving. Make a movement and sound to somehow express this issue.

3. Now this time don't make the movement, but simply feel a tendency to move. Then very slowly and with great feeling make this movement. Repeat this movement slowly until it takes you down to the essence of this experience.

4. Name this essence. Say how it is already an answer to your money issue and how you would apply this answer.

Another method I utilize these days when I am in any kind of tight spot or difficult situation I am having trouble coping with, is to begin walking the vectors of that situation. Arnold and Amy Mindell developed vector work as an adaptation of quantum physics to Process-oriented Psychology. There are two main ideas behind vector walking. The first is that we tap into the wisdom that all aboriginal people have known forever, that the Earth moves us and directs us. In vector work, we feel which direction the Earth turns us and moves us when we focus on a certain aspect of the problem, and we move in this direction. The second principle is that if we mark our starting and ending points after walking these vectors and we repeatedly walk with great awareness this beginning to end line, it will take us quickly down to the essence level. From this central or essence line, we can understand the meaning of all the other lines. We can use this method to work on dreams, and to work directly on money issues. The following begins with an exercise for working on our identity around money. After that is an exercise for working on money issues and how they apply to our relationships. Then another, for working on dreams (can be used to work on dreams about money). The final vector walk exercise is about money and its meaning in our lives.

EXERCISE: Vector Walks and Your Money Path

1. Find a place where you can walk freely, and mark your starting point. If you can't walk, you can do this with your fingers, or even imagination.

2. Ask yourself who you are these days in regards to money. Feel what direction this would move you in, and take a few steps in that direction.

3. Now ask yourself what is the best thing that has ever happened to you around money, and take a few steps in that direction.

4. What was the worst experience you ever have had, or what repeated difficult experiences have you had around money? Now walk in that direction.

5. What is the most surprising or mystical thing that ever happened to you around money? Now walk in that direction.

6. Now walk slowly, it may take you several times, from the beginning point to the end point of your walk. Feel into

this and come to the essence of who you are around money. When you are there, you will know, as you will feel it and you will be in absolute favor of the state you are in.

7. Lastly, walk this essence line while looking back at all the other lines and notice what you discover.

8. Make a note of all of this, and ask yourself how you can live this essence more in your daily life.

EXERCISE: Relationship Vectors and Money

1. Think of a relationship you had where money was an issue. What were the different positions/roles present? Who were you, what was your position? Who was your partner and what role did they play? For example, was one the provider, the other carefree, one the responsible, the other irresponsible, one was worried, and so on.

2. Who were (are) you in the relationship? Mark your starting point. Take time to let the Earth turn you in the direction that represents who you are. Take a few steps in this direction.

3. Who was your partner in the relationship? Take time to let the Earth turn you in their direction, and walk a few steps in their direction.

4. What was one of the most difficult money moments in your life? Feel the Earth turn you in this direction, and walk that vector.

5. What was one of the most ecstatic money moments in your life? Feel the direction of that vector and take a few steps in that direction. Mark this stopping point as the end point of your vector walking.

6. Now walk from the beginning point to the end point of your lines. Walk this slowly several times until you find the central line, central vector of who you are in the money world in relationship. You will find a deep quality, an essence of yourself that this line represents.

7. While walking this line, give yourself advice from this line about money, and specifically money in relationships, from the wisdom of your center line.

8. Now walk the center line while looking back at the other lines, and from this centered position, notice what insights you have into the other lines. How were all the lines that appeared to oppose each other actually connected?

EXERCISE: Dream Vector Work

1. Recall a dream, preferably about money.

2. Identify several symbols in the dream.

3. Mark your starting point and walk the line of the first symbol.

4. Continue to do this for each of the symbols you have chosen.

5. When you finish walking the lines of the dream symbols, mark your ending point.

6. Now slowly walk from the beginning to the end of your vectors, from the starting point to the end point. Walk this with a great deal of attention to what you are feeling until you can identify an essence, a place where all these other vectors spring forward from. State this essence.

7. Now try understanding how this essence line in itself is an interpretation of the dream.

8. Try to gain some guidance or wisdom in the financial realms from this dream.

EXERCISE: Money and Meaning

1. Mark your starting point. State your financial goals in concrete terms. Find the direction of this goal, and take a few steps in this direction.

2. Now state your deepest spiritual longing for yourself and the planet, and walk in this direction, mark this end point.

3. Now walk slowly several times between the beginning and endpoint, and feel into the essence of this line. When you get to the essence, feel it, move with it, and give a name to this.

4. Now walk the essence line while looking back at the other lines from the perspective of this essence.

5. How do your financial goals and your spiritual goals form a united front, a whole?

See if you get some ideas for new directions to take while walking this essence line, and make a note of this.

Process Work draws from the wisdom of many different indigenous traditions that use the Earth as a source of guidance and wisdom. In Process Work we utilize the Earth's wisdom to give us a sense of detachment. The Earth herself contains all the polarities, she is soft and hard, low and high, slow and fast, and all the other poles, therefore from this place of detachment we can work on all the different polarizations in our daily life. Earth based meditations are some of the most direct and powerful ways to get into this deeper wisdom we are calling Process Mind, this wisdom that we can access at the essence level. Mindell in his book Process Mind, says," Process Mind is the palpable, intelligent, organizing "force field" present behind our personal and large group processes and, like our deep quantum patterns behind processes of the universe. Process Mind is an attempt to extend and deepen our quest to know this field and these patterns as they are understood today in physics by connecting them to experiences studied in psychology and mysticism. (Arnold Mindell, 2010, p. xi) The more we practice letting ourselves merge with the Earth, becoming the mountains, rivers, oceans and trees, the more we can begin to bring this wisdom through in our lives.

What follows is a basic Earth based exercise, along with its application to money issues, and later, a more advanced application of this work.

EXERCISE: Earth Based Awareness

The purpose of this exercise is to practice finding our Earth spot and finding and being the energy that is present there.

1. Take a few breaths into your belly.

2. Now scan your body. This is a feeling-oriented scan. Notice where you feel most connected to your deepest self in your body. When you find that spot breathe deeply into this.

3. Take a moment to solely feel this spot. Now make a movement in one hand that represents this energy.

4. Associate this movement to a place on the Earth. What place on the Earth does this remind you of?

5. Go there in your imagination. Look around, feel the atmosphere. Smell the smells. Hear the sounds.

6. Now let this Earth spot begin to change and move your breath, allowing it to begin to move you.

7. Let yourself merge and become one with this spot.

8. Relax even more into this, let yourself go and let your altered state take you.

9. Bring this energy back with you into your body and your awareness as you come back to the room.

EXERCISE: Earth Based Work with Money Problems

The purpose of this exercise is to apply Earth Based methods to money issues.

1. Identify a difficult problem in your current or past relationship with money.

2. What disturbs you or is the most frightening or difficult part of this problem with money? Perhaps you have too little, you lose it all, hate your job, etc.. Identify the energy of this, such as too little, or too much struggle. Call that energy X energy and draw a line to represent the energy of that X, or make a motion of drawing in the air. For example, the feeling you can never work hard enough to catch up with your bills.

3. Now what is it that is most disturbed in you by that X energy? For example, maybe the part of you that feels life should be easier, or the part that wants to be debt free, etc.. Call this Y energy and draw the energy of that Y.

4. Take a few deep breaths.

5. Now scan your body, and sense where your deepest process is now in your body. Take a few breaths into this area.

6. Feel the place and make movements that express the feelings in this part of your body.

7. Now associate this with a place on the Earth.

8. Go to that spot in your imagination. Smell it, hear it, feel it, and become it. Let this Earth spot begin to move and dance through you as you become it.

9. Find out what the essential energy of this place is, and name the energy and awareness that emanates from this spot.

10. Be sure and make a note of this.

11. Now staying in Process Mind, in this deep place of oneness, and begin to tangle with this X energy and then the Y energy, helping them to dance together. Put the X in one hand and the Y in another, and let your hands move and speak and interact until you get to some kind of resolution.

12. If you get stuck at a certain point, let the hands begin to dance together and create a fluid power dance. Notice what comes up as the polarity disappears and this unified dance emerges. Give the energy of this dance a name.

13. When you feel the fluidity is restored, where the dance is happening, let Process Mind, your deepest self, advise you how to move forward in this relationship to money.

14. Make some notes on what is learned.

EXERCISE: The Wisdom of the Universe and Money Guidance

The purpose of this exercise is to access methods that make it even easier to connect to universal wisdom about our money issues:

1. State a money issue you want to work on.

2. Now begin to let yourself move. Let your arms swing freely and let yourself move with freedom, awareness and a sense of abandonment until you feel yourself going into a slightly altered state.

3. Follow those movements trying to happen. You might experiment with feeling connected to the whole universe and how it moves you, so you are not moving yourself but being moved.

4. Stay aware now, of your question about money and see how your question is answered during the movement process, or ask how the movement itself is an answer to your question.

5. Be sure to write down what you get as this kind of altered state material may leave as quickly as it comes.

| CHAPTER 4 |

My Story, Your Story Around Money

Each of us has their own story to tell about money in their lives. In our stories, we can discover and apply the truths of the previous chapters. I have mixed feelings in writing about my own life; in most of my books I tend to write about the experiences of my clients, friends, and others I know of. The information and supportive experience necessary for this book came from reading about other traditions and studying my clients, however, it primarily came through studying and experimenting myself, with my own dreams and life choices. I will begin by talking about my consensus reality, everyday relationship to money, providing some framework for how to examine and understand my subsequent stepping into the dreaming world of money. I would like to write a disclaimer, similar to the commercials that warn viewers to not try the following stunt at home. Much of what I did around the stock market that I am sharing in this chapter was extremely risky. I am writing about it so that I can illustrate how I followed my dreaming process through tricky, and at times treacherous waters. Nevertheless, if someone were to follow my process, it not being their own, they could be severely hurt in the markets.

This was true of my father, as well as a friend of mine who followed some advice, independent of his own individual process. He invested all of his retirement heavily in a few stocks, and ended up tragically losing it all. Even professional traders can get burned, or become addicted and unable to get out of the markets, for this reason be consciously alert in following your own individual process, and not mine. Your very own dreams and dream like experiences will help you to find your path.

Beginning Stages

As you read this, please be aware of your earliest experiences around money, and where they went from there.

Liking Money

My own story begins when I was a young child. I grew up in a wealthy suburb in St. Louis. We knew we lived in one of the least fancy neighborhoods in the area, which was one of the more wealthy areas, but as a child I never really knew much about the details of my family's economic status. Were we rich, middle class, struggling? It was hard to tell. I knew that we had enough, and that my grandparents would spend a great deal of money on us, making birthdays and holidays very special in terms of gifts. Therefore I thought my grandparents were rich, but did not know about my parents. I had a natural curiosity for and relationship with money. My parents bought me little banks that looked like pirate chests, and I would get very excited to fill them up with coins. My great grandmother gave us silver dollars, which I collected, and finally sold when I was in my late teens to help me get out on my own in the world. I never knew why I liked money, I just did, it was fun to have, collect, and earn. Yet, as I grew up, I also saw another side to money: I learned how it was not only associated with happiness, but also stress. As I grew older, I remember asking about what was upsetting my father, and my mother would say he was stressed about money. I remember him complaining a great deal about money—except when we went on vacation, then he would be much more relaxed about it. We all could hardly wait until vacation time came around.

Hating Money

Like many of my generation, my adolescence had many phases. My early adolescence involved a combination of playing with, and gradually learning to earn money. I worked for my father in his department store in sales as a summer job while I was in grade school and early college.. At one point, I helped him to realign his men's clothing department from clothes that had catered predominantly to older people, to clothes for young people-the population in his store's location that spent the most money on clothes. I also developed work skills through organizing book fairs, Christmas tree sales, and other functions at school. Then in high school, the Vietnam war and all the protests erupted. These protests coincided with the mindset of being against materialism. Suddenly, I realized that one of the large houses in our suburb was owned by the man who started the company making the napalm that was being dropped on innocent civilians in Vietnam. I became disillusioned, and started to hate the money world and everything about it. I felt that that world was somehow tainted. I especially despised the stock market. Mostly, because my grandfather who I had never been fond of, watched it all day—therefore I knew it must be evil. I went on to college and became a quiet radical in these views. I was certainly drawn to aspects of the counter culture, particularly those with emphasis on music, sex, love, and peace. I fought with my parents about politics non-stop, and we became increasingly distant. Dismayed, I went into therapy to find out who I was, and why it was that despite "having everything," I was so miserable at times in my life.

My experiences in college and a course I had taken there had opened me up to humanistic psychology, and eventually I went to live at the Gestalt Institute of Canada. This place had a combination of the strict awareness of a Zen center, and the freedom of a commune. Needless to say I was shocked, when, after driving the Camaro my grandparents bought me, along with my fishing rod, tennis racket, and a few other things, I was picked up at the dock of the island by a man with long hair in a jeep, who was both warm to me and snarled at all my goods. We drove to the center, and for the first time ever in my life, I saw women living there cooking naked in the kitchen and bathing in the ocean naked. Living there together, we encountered and confronted one another day after day, and learned how to get off the material wheel of the culture through becoming self-sufficient. We learned to grow and store food, fix our cars, heal our injuries and illnesses, build composting toilets, raise goats and chickens, and in other ways, we learned to survive and thrive without the almighty dollar as our main focus.

I learned to live on almost nothing. When I went back for a longer stay, a year later, I sold my Camaro to get there, and ended up with a 1959 Volkswagen pickup, that caught on fire a few times, and provided all kinds of other adventures. I was the first person living on the island to get a job permit and "commuting" job in town, and I walked miles every day to the ferry in order to go and work a counseling job.

Eventually, I was able to buy an inexpensive pickup, allowing me to drive to work, and was able to make enough money at the counseling job to pay my rent at the center. I had learned to drive without properly working car brakes until I could earn the money to buy new brakes.

One of the decisions I made on my first of four visits to the Gestalt Institute was that I wasn't going to be a lawyer, or go to the social work-law program my parents wanted me to go to, where I had already been accepted into. This program would allow people to move fluidly between the two fields, or find a kind of specialization, for example working in some kind of advocacy role as a lawyer. Instead I decided to be a social worker. This decision caused such a rift between my family and I that all family funding was cut off for college, as well as most all other areas of my daily life. I went from living an upper middle class young person's lifestyle, to a life of material poverty.

In this community lived some people who were very tight on money, as well as others from across the whole spectrum of wealth; I suddenly became part of the poorest people scraping by. Nevertheless, I was doing so much psychological and spiritual work that I felt less worried about life in general, including money, than I ever had through all the years of having money. At the time I was enthusiastically studying Gestalt therapy, Kabbalah, Native American spiritual approaches, kundalini yoga, and whatever else I could get my hands on.

Needing Money

When I left the center, as it had begun to fall apart, I did not know where to go next in my life. I took a break and went to live with relatives in Florida. After that I went back to St. Louis and decided to buy a Volkswagen bus, fill it with my personal belongings and my dog, and drive out to live in Oregon. I arrived with only a few hundred dollars to my name. Within the first week of arriving, I began to try and make enough to survive in two different ways. First, I started teaching a few classes at the local community college adult education program. This paid very little, but was a start. Next, I started buying coins for my cousin, who had a large coin dealership in St. Louis.

At times, I was so poor that I had to look all around for enough change to get gas to drive into town and teach my classes in Gestalt therapy and dreamwork. I began to notice that my constant money troubles were interfering with my spirituality. In the middle of my meditations I would become distracted by worries and thoughts of where I was going to get money for gas. Being poor was no longer simple and holy, it was becoming painful. When my Volkswagen broke down and I was told I needed a new engine, I began to cry. I sold whatever I still owned, and talked my father into letting me have some stock in my name to put up as collateral for a loan on the car. The car ironically ended up breaking down on a church parking lot. Something inside of me knew that I had come to the end of some phase in my material life.

Marriage, Family, Responsibility— on the Path to Dreaming

While my car was being fixed I was forced to find rides into town to teach, which was 30 minutes away. One day, while standing at the bus stop, I saw a man mailing a package. He was very nice, and I asked him if I might get a ride with him to Eugene. He said he would have to ask his friend BJ.

I assumed they were in a relationship, but it turned out that they were not, and his asking about the car had to do with something else. To my delight, almost immediately after meeting with her, it became clear that something was cooking between BJ and I. This was the beginning of a long dating, courting, marriage, close friend and co-parenting relationship. Today we are friends, who enjoy each other and still do various projects together, as well as coming together as family with our daughter. BJ was in much better financial shape than I was at the beginning of our relationship, and helped me out in several ways, including letting me and my nine goats move onto her property. She loved my spiritual nature, and for a while that was what I brought to the relationship.

Eventually, she and I both wanted more of an equally contributing relationship. A crisis hit one day when BJ told me that I should either open my own therapy practice, or get a job cooking at the local root beer stand in our small town. I decided to open my own practice, sharing a room located above the cleaners in a small town. Slowly, starting in this small town, and then also in Eugene, Oregon, a small city of about 100,000 people at the time, my practice began to build. I felt more and more responsible financially once I had my daughter, who I loved so much, as it felt joyful and natural to do whatever necessary to take care of her. Again, similar to the beginning of my life, money and I had a relationship that seemed inherently natural and positive.

There were a few huge leaps that took place in developing my practice. The first was when the school district came to me and offered me a job if I would go into the high school and work with their most difficult youth. I jumped at the opportunity, which ignited a long-term working relationship with the schools in the area. The next major development was that I applied for a grant for the county, and was awarded it. Suddenly, we, the counseling agency I had founded, were opening offices in three other small towns.

Our programs were bold, innovative, and achieved positive results. However, we were not very good at playing the political game and making the system that funded us very comfortable. We did not know exactly how to keep the county, our funders, happy. We assumed that if we simply did excellent clinical work we would be fine, but there were other important issues of paper work, presentation of our files and other areas we were not as strong in. When it came time to renew our grant, we put everything we could into the renewal, yet didn't get renewed. Suddenly, I found myself out of a well paying job. I owed my staff all kinds of money for vacation, sick days, and whatever they wouldn't be covered by future funding.

Furthermore, all of this happened at the time my marriage was coming apart. I needed to get my own separate house, and I took whatever money I had saved from my clinic director job, and put a down payment on a house. Then I found out I wasn't getting my funding from the state renewed. Suddenly I had a house with a big mortgage, no job or income, and growing debt. Financially, it was a terrifying moment.

Dreaming Arises

In response to all the demands now forced on me in managing the clinic, I had cut back my practice to about four clients. As I mentioned earlier in this book, in the midst of this crisis, I had a dream. Dr. Arnold Mindell, the developer of Process work, had taught me to follow and believe in my dreaming. In this dream, his father, who I had never met, showed up;

he told me not to worry about money and that it was taken care of. Within a few weeks, without putting out any advertising, or other effort, my practice began to grow. It doubled, then almost tripled within the next month. Except for a few slowdowns at the beginning, I have been full ever since, and this has been consistent now for probably about sixteen years. Of course, I furthered my studies and continued working diligently to improve my skills as a therapist, thereupon people did not simply show up out of nowhere without good reason in coming to see me. Nevertheless, the timing was uncanny; two weeks after a financial meltdown, something was there to pick me up and get me back on my feet again—I only needed to trust the dreaming process enough to move forward.

The same story theme surfaces again ten years later, when I entered the stock market, but we are not quite there yet. I am convinced that without this help from the dream-world, and my willingness to follow its advice and move forward with my practice, I never would have been able to handle the crisis I was in.

Arny Mindell has often told me that it is the crises themselves that open us up to these larger parts of ourselves; those more open to dreams and miracles. It is as if having some beautiful clothes that we never think much about, or use, yet because of a crisis, we go to the closet and take them out. They have always been there, existing, maybe even waiting for us to use them. This is how I experience this dreaming part of myself that is so connected to the universe. Ordinary reality, day-by-day drudgery, and other consensus norms and pressures cause me to forget about the beautiful clothes I have in the closet; that is, I forget that all I need to do is open up to my larger dreaming nature and the power of the universe is right there to show me the way.

The Stock Market as Zendo

The next developmental leap in my relationship to money started in the midst of a discussion I had with my brother, brother-in law, and sister. They were all talking about their investments, and how well they had done. I had a moment of enlightenment, suddenly realizing that I had slipped into the role of the poor but self-righteously spiritual one. I held on to my poverty as a badge of purity. In my moment of enlightenment, I became aware that this was a role I took on in the field of my family that limited my discovering my own relationship to money. I decided that I had experienced more of this role of being poor then I had ever needed, and was ready to make a change.

As much as I had hated the financial markets and world, I was getting myself ready to play. I was in a new relationship that was very different in the realm of money and spirit. I was with a partner who identified herself as very involved in spirituality, but not very strong in the area of money. My ex-wife had been very strong in the area of money and even though she was very spiritual, was just growing more into identifying herself as such. I was having dinner with my partner Sage's brother-in-law. He was talking about how much money he was starting to make through playing the penny stock market. I bought in, hook, line and sinker. I realized I could afford a million shares of a movie stock worth a fraction of a penny, and then just sit back and wait for it to hit a dollar and collect my million.

Of course, I ended up losing whatever I had put into the market, but learned a great lesson through this experience: I was no longer going to listen to any and every tip given to me, and I was going to invest in stocks of quality. I broke every rule in the book in getting started, including taking money out on a credit card backed check to begin buying. My personal criteria, was to buy stocks that would qualify in an ethical investing mutual fund portfolio. Ethical investing generally refers to stocks that aren't supporting war, environmental destruction and nuclear power. I spent about six months learning like this, and began to make money, especially once I learned to buy on margin. Buying on margin means that not only could I buy stock with the money I had invested but could borrow against that money. So if I had enough money to buy 100 shares I could borrow enough to own 200 shares. I was quickly learning when best to buy, hold, and sell from following the recommendations of professionals. Even so, I noticed how following the best of advice was often costing me money, and I began instead to combine these outer recommendations with my own intuition.

Soon I began to dream about the market. Nine out of ten dreams were fairly accurate about when the market would go up or down, and whether or not it would be in large or small amounts. Some days it was uncannily close to the exact amount the market or a specific stock would go up or down. I had trouble understanding why something as materialistic as the stock market would show up in what I considered the sacred realm of my dreams. Had I been wrong, and was there something dualistic still in my thinking, separating the sacred from the profane? It was a disorienting and mixed experience, as I felt thrilled about this new dream relationship with the stock market, while at the same time disturbed that I wasn't dreaming about much what I would call holy, only the markets, which I had hated so much of my life.

The next phase began when a relative of mine passed away, leaving me what for myself was a significant amount of money, even though it was still a small amount to play in the markets. She left me the money in the form of all the stocks I would have objections to, mostly chemical companies, and military stocks. I sold them, and bought more of my preferred type of stocks, for example, Whole Foods instead of Monsanto.

I kept learning, and slowly making money, until that infamous day in the fall when Google released its stock. I bought as much as I could afford, and the day they released their first quarter results, I had enough and was going to use it to send my daughter to college. I called on the phone the minute they announced the results, and told them to sell my stock as it was dropping. Unexpectedly, something went wrong, and the sale didn't work. I was furious and called back. I talked with a supervisor, and to my surprise, he told me that it had just gone back up, and instead of losing $18,000, I had made something like $38,000.

This sent me off to the races. In the next few days, I just about tripled the investment money that I started with, and should have sold out and walked away with it. Instead, I held on and Google began to sell off. By the time I finally sold my Google, I was still far ahead of where I started, but had now more or less doubled, rather than tripled my investment. For all that, something happened to me through making and losing such incredible amounts of money at once, something that I can only describe as getting hooked. I began to fight my way back, day trading, buying on margin in addition to using my day trading powers. I played Google every time they would announce their daily results. Sometimes I would win a great deal, and sometimes lose, but I never got back up to where I was that first win, and where I wanted to be.

I began to buy and sell many stocks, not just Google. Mostly I felt like I was peddling harder and harder, getting nowhere. I was waking up earlier and earlier in the morning, staying up later and later at night, and running out in-between therapy clients to sell in order to cover my margin, and so on. It began to be a nightmare. Finally, one day it went back up to where I could get out. I decided to give it one more day, and then again it plunged. I felt like I was on an emotional roller coaster.

My dreams seemed to stop coming, probably because I had stopped listening to them while back anyway. I was becoming obsessed with the goal of making back close to what I once had and then getting out. Three or four times I went through these cycles, especially with Google. I seemed to be losing my sense of timing. I just kept buying and selling, winning and losing, and wasn't going anywhere. I knew enough about addictions to know I was hooked, and I thought that I must use everything I knew to get myself free. I was starting to burn out from lack of sleep, on top of having an incredibly demanding career.

My health was beginning to suffer, as I was getting stomachaches that began in the morning as I watched the market. My relationship suffered, and in the middle of all of this, I was also trying to finish my PhD. Something had to go; I knew I could only carry on with this a short time longer before my relationship or therapy practice would begin to really suffer. I staying in good shape through running daily and training in the martial art Aikido at night, but I could tell that I was having trouble concentrating in Aikido, as well as in my practice. I was up when making money, that is, my mood was happy and optimistic, and when the markets dropped I became sad, depressed and worried. How could this be happening to me? I felt swallowed up by a foreign world, scared that any day I could lose it all, and be back to having nothing—even so, I could not get myself out.

I decided that I had to use my Process Work skills to examine what was happening. I saw my life spinning out of control and remembered again my deepest self and my Process Work skills that could help me get back to this deepest essence of myself. This launched me into an amazing journey, taking me into the most surprising discoveries. I discovered that I was not motivated in doing this primarily for money, but to complete certain pieces of my life that were necessary before I could move forward.

One of the biggest pieces was to complete something that my father had begun. He had made money, and then couldn't get out, and lost most of what he had earned. I had to understand what kept him involved in the first place, and what prevented him from getting out. I suddenly came to a clear understanding of the lure, the hook, and how difficult it was to get out. Without my connection to dreams and the dreaming realms, I don't think I ever would have been able to get out.

My father had his connection with me, but didn't have the support I had in being able to connect with and go into these worlds. I studied my feelings, body sensations, dreams, and every other piece of information I could acquire about myself, particularly focusing on the kinds of states I would go into. I found the part of myself that is self-destructive. No addiction can grow in soil that does not have elements of self-sabotage within. Why didn't I just let myself walk away, when several times I had the opportunity to leave with more money than I had ever had in my life? This awareness woke me up to so many ways that I don't take care of myself, from little things like not backing up important papers I am writing, to the subtle ways in relationships that I don't take care of myself.

The other side of an addiction that is important to recognize, is that there is something powerful fueling the addiction that needs to be integrated. I would go into a deep state through the addictive stock market playing: it was similar to the strong feelings of hope for a better life, those of making rapid and dramatic change, and especially of making great strides forward without having to work very hard. Since my early twenties I had worked with such intensity to earn money, along with so many other ways in my life I had strained and persevered. I had always pushed myself to my limits for good health and relationships, a solid career, success, etc.. There was something so enticing to me about the idea that I could make money without working very hard.

After much inner examination, I found this to be the powerful thing fueling my addiction that needed to be integrated. I had to work to integrate this sense of a less painstaking and more effortless, flowing, and enjoyable approach to living in all areas my life. Non-doing was calling me.

One example of integrating what had been fueling my addiction is of when I had been driving myself very hard to learn Aikido, practicing four days a week. With the insight I gained through the stock market experience, I make the decision to allow myself permission to practice whenever I wanted, and in doing so I have enjoyed learning Aikido far more ever since. My connections to my dreams also then began to come back, and I felt I could again follow my dreams out of the market.

Remember my previous story in this chapter about the Google crash I experienced. As I had just about made it out, there was one final unexpected crash. I had even told my mentor Arny Mindell that I was going to get out, I had only one more day of Google reporting, and on that day I would get out. I figured Google had never had a negative report, therefore my carrying out my plan should be a piece of cake.

That Thursday, I sat in my office on wireless, and watched Google have its first ever-bad report. I started watching it drop, and was sure it would bounce back. By the time that day ended, I had lost everything I had made since I began trading. I was back down to my original investment. I literally began crying, I just couldn't believe what had happened. I called a few friends, and began to come out of the shock. I kept saying, "I am exhausted, I can't fight my way back one more time." Yet, I knew I had to.

The way I had decided to get out prior to the drop, was by investing with a partner in a house at the Oregon Coast. It was a safe, great investment, as well as a fun place to be. Instead of stock market torture, I could enjoy my investment, and have a safe one. Suddenly, with this unexpected plunge, I didn't have enough money to make my payment.

The next morning Google recovered a little, and I immediately sold. I began to fight my way back, using other stocks and making a slow recovery. Essentially, I had to start from scratch. Having reached such a point of exhaustion, once I made enough back to pay my part of the coast house, I was intent on getting out immediately. To my dismay, this happened while I was camping, and I missed the narrow window to sell. I started to get depressed, scared, and hopeless.

A few days later, I was out on a river swimming and found many beautiful feathers on the ground. I took them home and made them into a Native American prayer symbol, which I hung on a tree right outside the window from where I started my stock market adventures at 5 in the morning. I prayed and prayed, and yet nothing changed. Every little recovery was pushed back by another problem.

Oil prices soared, and then, a few weeks before I had to get out to make the house payment, Katrina hit. I decided to go back to Google one more time, and a few other stocks that had faithfully bailed me out each time. A few weeks before I had to sell, the markets started a temporary rebound, as some of the news from Katrina wasn't as bad as previously thought. Then Google began to move. I was still far under any of my target totals to get out when I had the dream that freed me.

This dream was so important to me that I am repeating it here. There was a huge ship heading through a storm, and a little ship behind it. The little ship was in trouble, and had to get to a safe harbor. There was a possibility of safety, if the little boat could find the right harbor. Astonishingly, somehow the captain ended up picking the right number, which was something ending in the number 53. When I awoke, I felt encouraged and revitalized, knowing I was following something bigger, and was somehow going to be all right.

The following week I was at a seminar with my mentor, Dr. Arnold Mindell. Over a two-day period, Google and one other of my stocks went on a surge upward. I told myself that if my total got up to a number with the last two numbers being 53, I would sell everything and get out for good. I was still thousands of dollars away. The next morning Google surged and I was getting closer and closer to my anticipated total—it felt like watching a miracle unfold. Unfortunately, my computer kept going off-line.

I decided to skip the morning part of the seminar, and continue watching. Suddenly my total hit 53, and I immediately began to sell everything. I probably had fifteen stocks left, and I sold down to all but a few last stocks I didn't have many shares in. in stock. Suddenly I panicked, second guessing my plan, and went to the seminar to talk with Arny Mindell. I told him what I had done in following the dream thus far and selling at 53, but proposed that maybe I should go back in for just a day or two. He said to let it be, and to start enjoying life again. I took his advice and sold out completely.

In the days that followed, Google and the market as a whole started plunging again. Had I not followed the dream and Arny Mindell's advice, I would not have been able to get out in time to put my payment down in order for the house to be bought. For the next two months, I never looked at the markets. I felt like someone had let me out of prison; I had been both the jail keeper and the prisoner, and was now finally free.

Instantly feeling happier, I entered a long period of getting my energy back, catching up on sleep, recovering in many areas of my being and life, and of course, playing. Since this experience, I have never gone back in, except to keep a few small Chinese-based stocks for long-term, secure investments, along with some stable mutual funds I have had for decades. The days of the thousands gained, thousands lost, are over at last. I once had a few second thoughts, when I saw that Google had exploded upward—more than another hundred dollars a share. Perhaps I could have been able to take a few years off and write if I had stayed in, but then I also knew it still was continuously going up $50, down $60, and with such erratic leaps, I could have just as easily been burned all over again.

Overall, I knew that I had learned the important lessons I was to learn, and that I would never go back into this again as a trader. I had finished what my dad had not completed, which is to walk away in good financial shape, good health, and never go back. I had also made peace with my father. We had a fantastic relationship, and were very close—especially during the last fifteen years of his life. I shared with him what had happened to me in the markets, and how I had previously been holding onto confused and upset feelings at the fact that in the past he did not sell out of the market and distribute some of the money to his children, but instead kept going higher and higher. He then almost hit his target, which was more than he had ever imagined, and instantaneously lost most everything.

After myself having experienced the harsh reality, as well as the addiction in trading, I came to understand more of what my dad had gone through and was able to let go of any hard feelings I had about his past decisions. He had done the best he could in a world full of illusion and entrapment, and had chosen to stay in, doing what he felt would be best for his family. I still believe that it was part of what killed him.

His loss was tremendously stressful, and it wasn't that long after the big hit he took in the market that he developed the brain tumor that eventually killed him. I feel grateful to have gotten out alive and well, still having the rest of my life to carry on. As I look back now, the lesson of being able to detach and walk away was worth more than all the money I made. I had learned more about my ego and how I hate to lose, causing me to get hooked in.

Finally, this Zendo of the stock market taught me that there was something far more important than winning and losing, and that was following the process wherever it went. I learned about timing and learned again to follow my dreams and my path with intention and accuracy. Eventually, we all have to learn to let go of everything, understanding when and how to do this, and this experience was a great teacher.

This may sound like an indictment of the markets, but it is not meant to be. It is only that my fate, my path, didn't belong in the markets for too long a period. For someone else, a whole life trading could be fine. One of my friends is a professional trader, and plays the markets in a way that he feels is controlled, and an absolute money-maker. He will probably do this, he says, forever. More power to him. The key is to follow your own process and to know where or not and when to go into the markets, when to go further, when to retreat, when to hold, and when to exit. The only problem I had was when I became greedy and stopped following my dreams and my dreaming process.

If my dreaming process would have been to make millions and fund some peace efforts out of trading, I would have needed to follow it; if it were to take the losses and learn from the pain, I would have followed that. This is the key point here. It is not simply a "get rich scheme," although it can lead to that just as easily as it can to losing everything. One of the feelings I walked away with, and would like others to have, is that of empowerment. Rabbi Bonder said essentially that the potential energy for us to generate the money is present; we have our spiritual connections that we can turn into money.

It is important to take into account the societal conditions we live under, which regulate and restrict how much and what we can do, including the level of difficulty it may take. With this level of social awareness, we can use our dreaming process to successfully manifest money. Being able to make money through the markets somehow broke a long-time curse that I had felt around the agony of making money. As I got out of the markets, I realized that I could work an extra hour a day and make a good portion of what I had made in the markets, without any of the stress and harm. My process was to find a way to separate out how I had associated money with stress, and instead, connect money with flow, energy, and even relaxation.

Remember the opening quote from Lao Tse, expressing this sense that our job is to learn how to follow the flow. As my mentor Arny Mindell has said repeatedly, "learn to balance doing and non-doing." This was the antidote in getting off the wheel of gain and loss that I was had been so terribly caught on.

> "He who is attached to things will suffer much.
>
> He who saves will suffer heavy loss.
>
> A contented man is never disappointed.
>
> He who knows when to stop does not find himself in trouble.
>
> He will stay forever safe."
>
> *Lao Tse, in the Tao Te Ching, translated by Gua-Fu Feng and Jane English(1972, p.44)*

I was the one who needed to learn when to stop, as in Lao Tse's poem. Detachment was my real gain, and without it, I never would have gotten out with anything. Some of us need to do something like Zen meditation, Process-oriented Psychology, Aikido, Tai Chi or something similar in order to learn the balance between attachment and detachment, while others of us can learn from the stock market.

First you get into the market, then connect with and value money, for money itself and for the ease it can bring to your own life and the lives of others. Then get out of the attachment before it begins to take you over and control your life. You learn about greed and about how easy it is to focus on making money rather than sometimes addressing other sources of need in life, such as the need for space, creativity, relationships, relaxation, and spirituality. Money is a great place to understand the balanced and unifying way that spirit and matter can come together and support each other.

Zen koan: a question the master asks you with no apparent possible answer, and is meant to awaken you to a more enlightened state. The Zen master may ask you, "What is the sound of one hand clapping?" If you meditate on this apparent contradiction long enough, a moment of enlightenment will happen when all the opposites come together. Something deeper is called upon to get us out of this apparent trap of dualism. Being on one end of the spectrum for myself happened when I first moved to Oregon. I lived on about $400 per month, and spent most of my day praying and meditating in the forest, and milking and taking care of my chickens and goats, as well as having all kinds of exciting relationships to explore. Money was the least important part of my life, but nonetheless, haunted me like a hidden ghost continued to reappear every time the car broke, an animal became sick, or some other need came up.

In contrast, living at the other extreme: I was up at 5 or 6AM every day, putting in my four or more hours of watching the market ticker until I went to work all day, making many further trades by closing my office during my lunch break, and spending the evenings planning my next day's moves. Miraculously, in the midst of my misery, the spirit feathers I had hung outside my window and prayed through to help get me out gave me more than just that: they helped me to understand that the sound of one hand clapping was the oneness present through my deepest personal work, my spiritual guidance, my dreams, and my money situation.

The Kabbalists would call this concept a tree of life, with deep roots in the Earth, and branches to the heavens. In Process work, we call it taking a heaven and Earth approach to life, not either one or the other, but with everything connected. We call it staying connected to your Process Mind. Was my grandfather, who I had so much trouble with, trying to find God staring at that screen every day? Did my father only find God in the markets going up and being able to take care of us all? Did he later perhaps learn that God could also be found in the act of letting go? I saw him learning to let go in his dying process, and perhaps the stock market had been a big part of his learning to let go. These are koans I will continue to meditate on, ones that ask me to find the sound of that one hand clapping.

Current Life

I received a precious piece of enlightenment from this journey into the markets. The Buddhists say, before enlightenment, you chop wood and carry water. After enlightenment, you chop wood and carry water—*but something has changed in the feeling quality.* Presently, I still have to pay bills and find ways to make ends meet. I am continually working to find a balance in my cash flow, the balance between long-term savings and short-term financial needs.

What has changed significantly, is my level of anxiety around money has reduced by about ninety percent. Part of this is because there is more there; my investments in real estate will give me padding if I ever retire. However, the change is primarily in that the realm of money that had always scared me, causing me to despise it, no longer frightens me. Perhaps this can be compared to a mountain that is too terrifying to climb, or a ski run too terrifying to come down, that is, until you do it. When you do, it is still challenging, but the mountain is a mountain, and no longer a mountain of fear.

The original attitude I had as a child, of valuing money without making it too central in my life, is now returning. There is now time to focus on my relationship and my spirituality, as well as the ability to be present for my daily work in a happier and more positive manner. In fact, I now have the potential for even deeper concentration in all of these areas, as I do not have to spend time thinking about where I will get money for gas, rent or other necessities.

Several summers ago there were torrential rains that went in through the roof, ruining two walls and part of the wood floor in one of the rooms at home. I noticed the familiar old panic within me arise around how I could pay for the repairs, when suddenly a sense of calm came over me, reminding me that this was part of owning a home, just take care of it. Again, as a mountain is a mountain, a home repair is a home repair, and not the end of the world. On another occasion, the washing machine flooder our floors, causing a major disaster, but after all was said and done, we ended up staying in a wonderfully simple and accommodating hotel while much of our house was rebuilt for us in a style much closer to what we had originally wanted.

This isn't the end of the journey, but only as far as I have gone so far. Who knows where the end is, is it in death, or do we continue learning how to integrate spirit and matter in the worlds beyond death?

Remember in chapter three when you made your timeline about money in your life? As I made my own timeline, it became obvious that money for me was a place of growing understanding of the connection of the material and the spiritual. If I look back through the last twenty-five years, the worst day of my financial life was actually one of the greatest blessings. It was the day my Volkswagen bus engine blew. I had finally made it far enough financially to pay my bills while having enough food to eat, and was beginning to teach my classes on dream work and other subjects.

When the car engine blew, I was driving down a road and pulled into a church parking lot. I got out, looked at the engine and knew exactly what had happened. The oil plug had fallen out, and to drive a Volkswagen without oil meant the end of the engine. I felt like it was the end of me. In some ways it was, for this was a huge transitional moment. I found a way to finance the car repair, but while it was being worked on I had to find a ride—which ended up bringing me to the woman I would fall in love with, marry, and have my only biological child with.

That car disaster was nothing less than the next necessary experience in my evolvement, enabling me to move forward in my life. Later, when I lost an enormous amount of money in the stock market, the experience allowed me to realize that I had to move on, and could no longer find happiness in what I was doing. Spirit is behind everything that happens to us, although if you are like me, it can be most difficult to see this in the mundane, daily problems of life. Enlightenment for me, would be perceiving this Spirit to be just as present in the car breaking as it is in the mystical experiences I have out in nature.

CHAPTER 5

Family Issues and Money

Much of my work as a therapist has been with couples and families, and of all the issues that come up, money continues to be one of the most fundamental. In this chapter, I would like to take the time to unfold what is often behind these issues, and give some ideas about how to work with them in our own relationships.

Diversity and Money Arrangements

I have been fortunate to live in a city like Eugene, Oregon, which encourages people in following both traditional and non-traditional lifestyles on many levels. I have seen every possible form of money arrangement carried out between couples. Naturally, the most traditional approach is that of combining resources. Most alternative arrangements then work with various combinations of both sharing and having separate resources.

In the traditional approach, each person puts their earnings into one pot, and everything belongs to the both of them. This method offers many advantages, especially in that it is very simple to negotiate in certain aspects, and easier to organize. A more complex system, in contrast, is that of both partners maintaining separate finances while each contributes to joint expenses based on their ability to pay. The traditional path of both partners sharing everything corresponds easier with how the legal system would divide their resources, if the two happen to be legally married. This doesn't apply to couples not legally married by choice, or for gay and lesbian couples who are denied the right to marry.

Let us examine one couple's experience together in this realm: Sam and Shelia decide to come in for counseling together; they are fighting over money all the time. Sam thinks Shelia spends far too much. Both Sam and Shelia are stressed over money, as they have debts related to college loans and medical expenses. They are fighting over how they manage their shared resources. Even more, this situation is not as straightforward as may appear given the external circumstances.

Sam and Shelia are involved in a game that involves rank issues. Sam unconsciously carries more traditional ideas around family life, those that say the man makes the decisions around money, as well as controlling the purse strings. Shelia is resisting being controlled, and while not having power in this traditional source of rank, she is very powerful in terms of being able to use money as a weapon to get Sam's attention. When Shelia feels neglected, she spends more and more money. Our work is to get to the bottom of why Sam does not give Shelia the attention she needs, and why Shelia does not deal with this issue directly with Sam, rather than sabotage their finances. Hence, even though the external structure of their financial troubles may appear straightforward, commonplace, and less complex given their traditional method of combining everything they have, the deeper issues behind the problem presented remain complex and need to be unfolded and worked with.

In another example, Jim and June are in a non-traditional financial relationship. They are both professionals, each having their own separate accounts in addition to a joint checking account. Each of them puts a certain amount of money into the account to cover their combined expenses. Jim makes more money than June, and the way they work this difference out, for example, is that if Jim wants to go on a vacation that June says she can't afford, Jim will pay the portion she can't afford.

The advantage to this system is that Jim and June both feel free to spend their money on what they want, as they are supporting each other to be more independent. However, the difficulties are in the rank differences this creates. Jim lives a much plusher, comfortable lifestyle than his partner, and this creates hostility that causes disputes between the couple. Jim drives a new sports car, while June drives an older standard model. He buys himself much of whatever he wants, and is generous and buys her presents, but June must be much more careful with her finances. He feels more secure than she does, because of his financial backing. Every time they want to make a purchase beyond what they have allocated for in their joint account, they have to discuss it and work out who pays what, which is time consuming and difficult at times. Jim wants to hold on to the system, as he feels safer knowing that he doesn't have to deal with her past and recurring debt. Yet both suffer with the tension of this economic disparity.

It is hard being a well-off tourist visiting an area where one sees great poverty, but in many ways much more tricky to handle economic disparity within one's own household. People in this kind of relationship often talk about how their living with such a separation between their finances makes them feel less united and close—less like a team. It is necessary to do in-depth work on these issues so that we might find the most complete and optimal common ground, one that offers independence as well as closeness, and safety and security for both parties.

Issues of independence and dependence, and togetherness and space are some of the most difficult issues that plague relationships—and money happens to provide an intense and tangible way to face and work on these issues. Both positions, the one that identifies with and desires more separation, and the one that identifies with and desires more togetherness, are roles that can change throughout the course of a relationship, even through the course of one day.

Most of us have found ourselves in either one or both of these roles several times in relationship. It may be difficult to see while playing either of these, but both roles are limited and contain blind spots. Those who identify as separate in the financial realms risk being unable to see how their individual actions, and the actions of their partners, are related.

In another situation, Fred argues that his money is his own and he can spend it any way he wants. However, this mindset may prevent him from noticing the feeling reactions his partner Jane has when he exclusively spends money on himself and/or his daughter, her stepdaughter. Reversely, Jane sees their relationship as being more together, as one unit, and therefore desires for their money to be in more of one mutual pot than Fred believes it should be. Jane would like them to be more of a couple, and she holds on to the high dream that even though Fred has much more money than she does, it is really both of theirs. She is shocked that when they begin to talk about divorce she finds herself in real financial trouble.

Fred's view is that their marriage issues have nothing to do with money issues. He had been clear all along about their financial separateness, but failed to notice the jealousy this brought up in Jane, especially when she was in times of great financial stress. Moreover, he hasn't a clue to how this has affected their sex life as Jane's wounding shuts her down in more and more ways. Both are suddenly in a position of being hurt by their lack of clearly perceiving the relationship. Being in the position of having more or less money may affect your perception of how the money relationship should be structured.

When I was the one with much less money than my partner, I would jump on any suggestion that she might be sharing or giving me some more of her money, as I wanted to see it as "our money." When I was the one with much more money in a relationship, I held onto my separateness so as to protect my finances from my partner's debt and self-destructive pattern of creating more debt. This was what a former partner had said to me, that she needed to hold onto her money in order to protect herself and us from self-destructive patterns of running up debt.

Both of these positions contain high dreams, dreams of what I would have liked to happen, which often times have very little to do with the outer reality. When I was with someone wealthier than myself, I was always dreaming that out of a combination of love and natural desire to take care of my needs as a partner would, she would jump in and do this for me financially. She often did, but my dreams were of receiving even greater financial generosity.

Throughout adulthood I have had many people in my life promise me money, so many that if they had in fact followed through, I would easily be able to do nothing but write books on psychology all day long. When I finally realized these were my high dreams that didn't fit the outer relationship reality, I was able to take far better care of myself, and my relationships. Like most people who maintain separate finances and are in the position of having much more money than their partner, I would dream that my relationship and my partner's feelings wouldn't be affected much by this disparity in our financial lives.

Again, this was nothing but a high dream. In my experience, I was very generous with my partner, yet I could see how often she felt hurt and disturbed by the disparity. Money is so intertwined with human emotions that viewing financial issues solely as material-based transactions is a major setup for relationship problems.

Different systems of psychology support these different roles of separateness and togetherness. When I studied Gestalt Therapy, we used to recite the "Gestalt Prayer" written by Fritz Perls. We would say something to the degree of, I am I and you are you. I am not in this world to live up to your expectations and you are not in this world to live up to mine. It was a guiding principle, like a biblical verse.

In Process-oriented Psychology, we identify relationship as this separateness, but also together in a far more subtle and complex aspect. Yes, there is a distinct "I" and a "you," but there is also the way that I *am* you and you *are* me. We share certain characteristics, including our ways of being with money. Then there is the "We," the part that is both of us together. We call this the Relationship Body, or the Relationship Dreambody.

The next time you are sitting with a couple, try and look first at each individual, and then also at the space in between the couple, the shared space, and you can get a sense of something that is both of them together. This is the position that I am most interested in looking at when I work with a couple: the kind of joint growth they are involved in together, and how each of their own individual growth is related to the other.

This is also part of "systems thinking," which is the basis of a kind of family therapy, a view that whatever an individual experiences is both important and related to the whole. Systems theory focuses on the role of the individual as part of a whole system affecting the system and being affected by the system.

Another good way to access these different parts of relationship, and the whole that they make up together, is to work with walking these different parts as vectors. Recall that vector walking is a way to reach the sentient, or deepest shared level of experience. The parts include who I am, who you are as my partner, who we identify with as a couple, and who we don't identify with as a couple, the "not we." This moves way beyond the complexity of I am I and you are you. The "not we" is the part of the relationship beyond the conscious identity of the couple.

For example, let us say that I ask a couple who they are, and they respond saying that they are dear friends and lovers. I tell them that this sounds wonderful, and then proceed to ask them who they are *not* these days as a couple. They both respond that they are not fighters, for they never conflict. This reveals that the fighter's role of the relationship is still a mystery that is unknown, unexplored, and missing. There is the potential for all kinds of excitement and growth if we could bring this in as well.

To illustrate, lets us look at another relationship. Steve and Paul have been in a long-term homosexual relationship for years. When I ask them who they are together around money, they both say they are doing pretty well and are somewhat financially secure. When I ask who they are *not* these days around money, they say that they are not a couple who fights over money. Consequently, within the "not fighting" lies all kinds of issues that are perhaps being avoided, issues that if faced and went into, might make them feel even more secure together.

A more Process-oriented approach to combining money in a relationship would be to integrate feeling issues into the structure, and to let this evolve over time. As couple grows to trust each other more and love one another on a deeper level, their financial relationship needs to somehow reflect this. This does not mean that the financial arrangement changes every other day based on how a couple is feeling, but that these kinds of changes can either just happen naturally over time, or couples can re-evaluate together as a kind of periodic practice.

Some couples rush too quickly into sharing their finances, only to become nervous and fight over the issue, often leading to one or both of them getting burned when they separate. Other couples unite all other aspects of their lives, waiting until they both have a clear understanding of and feel secure in becoming more involved financially together.

Due to the elements of unconscious rank and individual past trauma, it is hard to be, let alone remain aware of money issues in relationship. I personally had to go to a friend recently to seek advice about my own money arrangements with my relationship partner. I had been following a model that many of my therapist colleagues in Eugene were following, as well as many of my clients and friends.

While this may be true, my partner felt this model to be unfair and one-sided. I went to a friend who is incredibly progressive on issues like this; she told me I was stuck in a kind of rigid thinking which prevented me from really hearing my partner. My partner detested this model. She felt it put her down in some ways and forced her into more financial independence than was right for her body and her energy. I could not hear her though, because I had heard such great things over the years about this model and believed them to be true for our relationship. I then went back to one of my friends, who had told me in the past that this model had worked amazingly well for their relationship. This time I spoke with her about it, she laughed and said they had given it up years ago. I decided to make a change, and opened up to what my partner wanted.

Through doing this I have found that both my partner and I are happier with a new and more open sharing system. I have the opportunity to truly feel my power and joy in being a provider, while still being able to set my limits and follow my feelings. She contributes a lot as well, but has stopped overworking and instead spends more time in her art and spiritual work. Our relationship dynamic now has a sense of relaxation it has never had.

The point of this illustration is that sometimes we need to go outside of our system, our belief systems as maintained in our family, our relationship, and even our friends, in order to find clarity and perspective we need. This feedback will in turn help us stay conscious of our rank and our belief systems, along with finding unexpected and creative solutions that answer to our unique situations perfectly. I had helped many many couples through this kind of conflict, and finally needed to get this kind of help for myself. It is important to fight one's own resistance and not be shy around couples and family money issues, as it is tricky ground and we need each other's help to stay awake around this.

EXERCISE: Vectors, Relationships and Money

Here is an exercise for walking these different parts of a relationship, and seeing where your process is at currently:

1. Mark a place on the floor as your starting point.

2. State who you are in your current relationship, in regards to money.

3. Let yourself take some steps in the direction that this part of you feels moved or pulled toward.

4. Now say who you think your relationship partner is, with regard to their position around money.

5. Make some movement in the direction that you feel the Earth is moving you toward when you think about their position.

6. Now ask yourself who you are together in this relationship when it comes to money, and walk that vector.

7. Ask yourself who you both are not in regards to money and take a few steps in that direction.

8. Finally, mark your ending point where you have stopped. Slowly begin to walk from the place you marked as your beginning point to the ending point. Walk this slowly and feel into what is under this line, the deepest feelings and awareness that comes to you while you walk this line. Keep walking it until you can give a name to this essence of your financial relationship.

9. Now while walking this essence line, look back at all of the other lines, and see what you have learned, what new perspectives you have gained about your partner and your relationship.

10. Share this with your partner. Ask them to do the exercise and compare notes with you.

11. Talk about how these insights might help you to make your financial relationship more conscious, and talk about what you can learn about the rest of your relationship issues from having worked on this one together.

Here is a shortcut method:

1. Mark your beginning point. State who you are in regard to money in this relationship, and walk this line or vector.

2. Have your partner do the same, walking the line representing who they are. The partner's line starts at the point your first line ends, and where the partner stops, mark this as the end point.

3. Now have both of you walk from the beginning point to the end point, slowly, and together find an essence of the financial relationship. Then discuss this new insight with one another.

Family and Cultural Ghosts

What looks like a battle between two couples is more often than not, a battle between two family systems not being identified, and even two different cultures. Here is an example of unidentified family systems, or family ghosts. One person's family was very poor and in order to survive, they developed a sense of rigid discipline and stoicism. The other person in the relationship came from a wealthy family where they were never denied anything wanted/needed. Of course these two systems are going to collide when these two people become partners.

When systems collide, it is difficult for the couple to have a sense of detachment and broader perspective around the situation. Rather than taking the conflict and differences personally, this kind of objective and detached position would more effectively support them in understanding what is happening between them. Out of discomfort and fear, each person condemns the other's system, defending their own way of being without much awareness as to where their approach came from.

For example, Sandy and Kathy have been in a relationship for several years. Sandy came from an impoverished background, and even though she now has a great job, she is always saving every penny she can for the disaster that might be coming. Kathy loves to live well. She enjoys the sense of economic freedom from stress that growing up in her wealthy family brought her. Both live in and share the same European culture.

Sandy judges Kathy as impulsive, self-indulgent, and spoiled. Kathy thinks Sandy is uptight, stingy, and neurotic about money. Without really understanding where each other's approach comes from, they are quick to condemn the other, and their relationship suffers from this polarity. Our therapy work involves my uncovering and representing these different family attitudes and experiences, and helping the two process what comes up.

At one point, Sandy shares about when her family was running short on money for food, and how she had to wear only hand-me-down clothing that some of the other schoolmates made fun of. She begins to cry, and Kathy holds her. Kathy momentarily has compassion on her partner after hearing her life experience and understands where she is coming from. In another session, Kathy talks about how it was to live with so much material wealth, without having much family closeness. She shares her sadness about how money so often became a substitute for love, and how painful this is. She realizes that one of the main ways she nurtures herself is through spending, but that she still feels empty and unloved.

Piece by piece they grow in understanding each other's views and experience around money, and as they begin to discuss what they could learn and gain from the other the most amazing transformation happens: Sandy talks about wanting to be less uptight and reactive around Kathy's spending, and Kathy wants to focus more on love and less on spending, and also to use some of her economic rank and inheritance to help Sandy feel secure and help heal the years of economic trauma caused by her history of low income.

Both discuss their desire to break family patterns; Sandy wants to create wealth and a comfortable lifestyle for herself, no longer following her family's poverty path, and Kathy wants to breakthrough barriers around getting the emotional love she needs to give and receive. Both made phenomenal progress in learning to understand and appreciate each other's essence that they brought to the financial part of the relationship. They were both able to see that they needed some sense of healthy discipline and frugality, to consciously save for what they wanted, as well as more of a sense of freedom from worry and struggle, allowing them both to relax and enjoy their lives.

Going beyond family ghosts, let us explore how cultural ghosts come into play with relationships. Jeff and Lisa had been married for five years and lived on the East coast of the United Sates. One of their biggest ongoing fights was over Jeff's career. He was a brilliant man with many different personal qualities and skills, and his career was beginning to take off. However, Lisa would criticize him for how long it was taking, and would sometimes tell him that he would never bring in the kind of income she and the children needed to have a comfortable life. Jeff would defend himself with both his good intentions, and with facts and figures showing his progress. Jeff would tell Lisa that she was just like her mother, always criticizing her father around money and being obsessed with not having enough.

When we went into this more deeply, I played the role of the mother, and told Jeff what a loser he was financially. Immediately, Lisa went and stood by Jeff and defended him against this externalized version of this mother who through Lisa was disturbing the relationship. However, this didn't really move things, as Lisa went back to her old position with Jeff quickly, so we went deeper and explored where the mother was coming from.

Lisa explained that her mother came from a country and a historical period where people had gone through terribly hard times during World War II and had been very poor and hungry. So it wasn't just Lisa's mom that was organizing Lisa's behavior, but the whole culture her mother came from and represented. I played out various roles and voices from this culture, and suddenly both Lisa and Jeff had tremendous compassion for these voices of desperation. Their relationship problems were representative of a wound, a trauma that had happened to her mother and her mother's people, and somehow the depth of this whole experience seemed to transform both Jeff and Lisa. The polarities they were experiencing around money then dissolved through this deeper understanding.

I can identify with this issue personally. I could not understand my father's relationship to money for example, without understanding what it was like to go through the Depression in the United States, and be forced to quit school to try to support your family. These kinds of feelings and deeply rooted beliefs surrounding money cannot be changed without profound psychological work and reflection.

I know many people who grew up poor, and still live as if they are poor, even if they have millions of dollars. One's material reality may change, but not necessarily their emotional reality around money. Families can pass on attitudes about money for generations without knowing where the attitude came from, and without ever processing it.

EXERCISE: Cultural and Family Influences on Your Relationship to Money

Here is an exercise to try to understand how to work with this in yourself and in your relationships:

1. Think of a time when you have been upset, anxious, panicky or furious about money, with yourself or your partner.

2. Recall the details and try and feel some of those feelings now. Make a note of what feelings are present.

3. How are these feelings influenced by your family's attitude and experiences with money?

4. How are they influenced by the larger culture you live in, or your family's and your cultural background?

5. Try and act out some of these family and cultural voices.

6. What kinds of trauma and issues are unresolved in the background in family and culture? Think of something you could do that is creative that might help resolve these.

7. Now imagine that you had healed the trauma, wounding or other difficulties that were there. Act for a few minutes like someone completely free of these influences, and notice what it feels like. Note what would be different about you and your life if this were you now.

8. Give a name to this new kind of attitude you would have if free of these other influences, and think about where in your life you could use more of this attitude.

| CHAPTER 6 |

Addicted to Money

Money can become a powerful addiction. We can be addicted to making money, hoarding money, spending money, poverty, gambling, losing money (through a variety of ways, such as poor investments and compulsive spending) and so forth. In Process Work, we identify and work with two different points on the addiction spectrum, addictive tendencies and full-blown addictions. An addictive tendency is a pull in a certain direction that is powerful and may someday turn into an addiction, but is not considered harmful at the present stage.

For instance, Sue works very hard at work. She has a clear goal of obtaining a certain level of income in her life. She is clearly on the way to the goal, and keeps this in balance with the other needs in her life thus far. However, her best friend Randy works at the same law firm, and wants to earn twice as much as Sue. Randy works all night, and is looking more and more haggard. She is going up the scale, but her health and her relationship are starting to fall apart. She is beginning to also abuse some of her prescription medicine to help her stay up nights and get by without sleep. Randy is headed down the path of addiction. She is experiencing harm in several areas of her life.

When this kind of focus on money begins to have severe negative consequences in one or more areas of her life, then she has an addiction to money. I would call this a positive addiction because it follows along with society's values, unlike a heroin addiction, which goes against society values. Positive addictions are more difficult to address, as the entire culture the person is submerged in may be supporting this direction. It might be hard to notice that she is slipping, as many people at times look that haggard, or drink a few too many or take a few too many pills.

I once asked a client of mine about his drinking habits that were part of the socializing around his job, and he said that it was not a problem, that everyone from work went out together a night week, and they became much more drunk than he would. When he slept with someone in violation of his marriage and didn't even remember that he did this, he finally realized that he had a serious problem. Money can be a real rush, a high to be enjoyed; however it is easy to get hooked on this high to the point that we marginalize the other parts of our lives.

What can we do if this begins to happen? The basic approach to addictions through Process Work is to find the essence of what is fueling the addiction, and then find beneficial ways to replace the harmful behaviors connected to the addiction. For example, Paul is gambling away his family money playing video poker. When he plays, he feels powerful, as though he can beat the system.

This power is the essence of what is fueling Paul's addiction, and is something he needs; if he could actually harness this power and use it constructively, he could have the energy he needs to create a more positive work scene, which would in turn bring him more money. Paul is similar to how I was when I was caught in the stock market. By channeling the essence of my addiction into a positive direction, I realized I could do almost as well financially if I would just see one additional client a day, instead of four hours of agonizing stock market winning and losing.

Janet has a shopping addiction, and when she shops, she feels like she can finally nurture herself instead of her family. She buys and buys until she is in serious credit card trouble. Her buying is fed by something positive, that is to really nourish herself in the midst of taking care of so many others. However, her methods aren't working in that after the high of shopping comes down, she is left with outrageous bills and horrible fights with her husband about spending and money. She then ends up feeling bad about the fights, guilty about the spending, only to turn again to shopping to help herself feel better.

This is why I call this chapter getting off the wheel, because addiction to money is and endless cycle. You gamble, lose, feel terrible, borrow more to try and make up, then lose more, borrow more, and suddenly you have gotten yourself in real trouble. The way off the wheel is not in winning big, because that only reinforces the addictive cycle again.

The only way off is to wake up to the nature of the addiction and find a more effective way to take care of yourself, to feed and channel the essence of what keeps the addiction alive in a healthy way, without using a "fix" that is only temporary and destructive. That immediate fix can be overwhelmingly seductive, as it promises that you will feel good fast. We say the heck with consequences, and give in, only to find ourselves right back to facing the negative consequences."The draw of the addiction is similar to someone who sells us a false bill of goods, and we fail to read the fine print of what we will end up paying for what we thought was too good to be true."

EXERCISE: Breaking Money Addictions

Here are a few practical exercises to help break money addictions:

1. Remember a time you felt addicted to money, and were spending in an out-of-control manner. What was the harmful aspect that made it addictive?

2. Now imagine you are about to indulge in this addiction. Go into detail in your imagination, include all of your senses, and see if you can notice the signals that go along with pleasure, and the momentary excitement or relief of indulging. Try to catch a movement signal in your body, and amplify this signal. For example, maybe you clap your hands, or lean back and relax and look up at the sky.

3. Keep expressing this signal and continue to do so even more until you find out what is trying to express itself here. Give this a name and then see if you can go deeper and get to the essence of this signal. Repeat the movement signal over and over again, very slowly, until you can feel into this essence. Give this essence a name.

4. Talk from this essence, this centered place within yourself, and advise the addicted part on how to transform and break this addiction. Make a movement that goes along with being free of this addiction.

5. Talk or write about what life changes would go along with living from this essence, instead of feeding the addicted part.

| CHAPTER 7 |

Beyond Addiction— Finding Freedom in a Material World

Scarcity and Abundance Consciousness

In the section on social action, we went into great detail about the disparities that exist worldwide between the rich and poor. Contrarily, this section is not about outer material realities but inner psychological realities. At times people, communities, organizations or businesses carry a poverty-consciousness, even if their number of profitable opportunities or their wealth is significant. This refers to a mindset that sees poverty and feels poverty whether or not there is really poverty present. It is often the result of some kind of trauma around money in the past that makes it impossible to be in the here and now with what is present.

A common and clear sign of this poverty-consciousness in individuals is that they are constantly anxious and striving when it comes to money. There lacks a sense of centeredness, thereby any unexpected expense or change can be traumatic. The language often used by those with this consciousness includes such statements as, "You never know what could happen," "You can't count on this," and "Yes, I have several hundred thousand, X million dollars, etc., but in *today's world*, this simply isn't much."

The relationships in a scarcity model are often what I call a shark tank or feeding frenzy. It is the feeling that there is a bowl of spaghetti, many hungry people, and not enough to go around. People begin to spar over things, and this becomes a way of being. It was only yesterday that I found myself discussing with a colleague about how businesses have different consciousness levels like this. Businesses that perceive themselves as quite wealthy often carry a sense of ease around negotiations. As my colleague had shared of his experience, it is far easier to be in a cooperative mode than a competitive mode.

Groups with scarcity models bring out survival issues for people, while groups with abundance models shift people out of survival mode, where it is easier to think about and care about the well being of others as well as oneself. Through an abundance model people can live their lives with less stress and more ease. In this privileged position, one is able to focus their attention and energies on abundance—allowing for much greater creativity and flow.

In the Process Work community where I teach, we process these issues together often. Several years ago we worked on competition, and discovered that we were in our own kind of feeding frenzy, based on a sense that there was not enough to go around. Now there really were not enough students for all the classes to thrive, but the more important factor at play was the state of consciousness we held, our focus and how it was affecting our workplace. I for one would sign up to teach everything possible, and then afterwards would ask myself why I had done that, as I may have signed up for much more than I even wanted to teach—I had found myself caught up in the frenzy.

In contrast to this is my learning from my partner Sage. When we first got together over ten years ago, she was finishing graduate school as a marriage and family therapist. At the time we had a conversation that we often refer back to, even now. While walking around a beautiful lake in Oregon, we were talking about our careers. I wanted her to get her career off the ground because I didn't have enough money to support her and her child, and I didn't want to have to support her. I told her I knew a great deal about starting a practice, as I had built a rural counseling clinic, as well as a private practice from the ground up.

To my surprise, Sage responded by telling me that she wasn't going to approach things the way I did, but in her own way, and that this would mostly involve meditating and manifesting clients. We had an intense fight around the issue, as I told her that her methods were only a small part of what would be necessary for things to come together, and that she had to do the hard work of all the steps of building a practice.

She stayed firm in her decision, saying that she was not going to do it that way, and that I should wait and see. I felt like I had gotten involved with a woman who was so very dreamy and astral, that her feet would never come down to the Earth enough to build a practice and help us out financially. Yet over the last ten years together, I have witnessed her magic work over and over again. She completely shocks and frightens me by taking off a great deal of time in the summer and I see her caseload dropping. Then she does what she calls her manifesting exercises, and her practice fills within a few weeks.

This phenomenon is unheard of in my experience, where it is believed to and does take most of us years to build a practice. Sage simply puts her intention out there and it comes to her. As I reflect on this while writing, I realize that I had encountered a similar experience of this faith and effortlessness when I built my practice. It was when I had the dream that assured me in the midst of disaster that everything was taken care of, and sure enough, my practice took off. Yet I am examining Sage's techniques because hers is a much more conscious process, while for myself the experience had just come as a gift from the dreaming world.

In this section I will include some of her abundance exercises, however, one must note that a large determining factor in their success is in having the firm belief and awareness that the universe is infinitely abundant and gives us that which we ask for. I have seen many different examples of abundance work in addition to what Sage does. I was once at a workshop with a shaman from Africa. He taught us an exercise involving tying knots into a rope, and putting into the knots our intention to get what we wanted. One of his students told me that the first time she did this, she put in that she needed $35,000 for a down payment to start a healing center. Within a week, someone came up and offered her the money.

I have heard so many different stories like this of people being given money, houses, and had all kinds of other dreams fulfilled. In fact, in a way, the house I'm sitting in now while writing my book here at the Oregon coast was just like these stories. I had always had a dream to have a house here by the ocean, although I couldn't see how it was possible. Yet before I knew what was happening, it appeared and came to me. The whole thing happened like magic. I had a dream, made a few phone calls, and poof, suddenly this house became available, and it is now ours. If someone had told me a few years prior, that I would co-own a house at the Oregon coast, I would have laughed at them, but after experiencing this magic for myself, I do not doubt the reality of such miracles manifesting before our very eyes.

Part of scarcity consciousness comes from earlier life trauma, as well as family and cultural trauma; again, I have seen clients completely anxious about money who have somewhere between a million and a half to more than ten million dollars. All the while, this concept of abundance consciousness seems to transcend material financial realities. Abundance consciousness can be both a gift that some people already have, and something that can be practiced and cultivated. I make it my practice to remember to ask the universe for what I need, however, but in my acknowledging a greater wisdom than my individual self present, I remain conscious to manifest what I want as it is in harmony with this universal flow, will, or direction. Referring back to the Kabbalistic Rabbi's words, there is this great spiritual reservoir of energy that each of us can draw from what we need, if we have the right intention and we know how to do this.

One of the popular resources teaching how to get off the wheel of money addiction—the mindset and lifestyle of never having enough to feel secure—is a book written by Joe Dominguez and Vicki Robin called *Your Money or Your Life*. The author's main argument is that the way we are organizing our money lives does not work. We have bought into illusions that we if only give up our lives and tow the line, working hard, often at jobs we cannot stand, we will make it financially, be secure and happy.

Dominguez and Robin list a many statistics to back up these ideas, and here are just a few of their key statistics that reinforce how we are stuck on the wheel: The average amount of money saved for retirement, emergencies, and the like for a person in the Untied States at age fifty is $2,300. Furthermore, 48% of 4,126 male executives saw their lives as "empty and meaningless" despite years of professional striving (1992, p. XX). This is now old data but still relevant in what it reveals about our culture. Fast forward 20 years to this year; I was searching the web I found that without adjusting for inflation, according to The Employee Benefits Research Institute 2009 Research Confidence Survey, more than 53% of all American families of all ages have less than $25,000 in all their savings and investments.

The authors continue on to explain that we can get off the wheel through cultivating what they call FI thinking, or Financial Intelligence, which they define as "being able to step back from your assumptions and your emotions about money and observe them objectively."(1992, p. XXV). FI thinking involves a special kind of detachment in relationship to money issues through with which one can achieve financial integrity."Financial integrity is achieved by learning the true impact of our earning and spending, both on your immediate family and on the planet."(1992, XXVI). The goal of following the steps in *Your Money or Your Life* is financial independence, which they say, "is the totally natural, and inescapable, by –product of life."(1992, XXVI).

Dominguez and Robin examine the high costs of modern life when they share of psychotherapist Douglas LaBier's work: "The steady stream of "successful" professionals who showed up in his office with exhausted bodies and empty souls alerted him to the mental and physical health hazards of our regard for materialism."(2002, p.5)

They also highlight how the materialistic view of unlimited expansion is hurting our planet of limited resources; this damage is shown through pollution, global warming, and other ways we are abusing the planet.

One of the key points that these two make is that of how it is now considered almost a patriotic duty of citizenship to keep shopping until we drop. Consumerism for the authors is like a growing cancer. We came from a healthy system in which our sense of fulfillment appeared when our basic needs were covered. However things evolved to this modern living place where we believe that money is the key to fulfillment, so we can't say when enough is enough. There is no longer a natural state of healthy satisfaction; we are like horses, who, if left to get into the grain, will eat until we kill ourselves.

As with many of the abundance books I will mention further along in this book, these authors have a plan. Step one is called "Making Peace with the Past," which begins with taking a cold hard look at how much money you have made, and what assets and liabilities you have. Part of this process is to look at the four different perspectives on money: The first is the practical and physical realm. The second is the emotional, psychological realm. This realm includes looking at our family backgrounds around money, and looking at money as it really relates to security and power, as well as social acceptance. The third is the cultural realm—seeing how money is part of a specific culture, conditioned by cultural forces. The fourth realm is personal responsibility and transformation, where we open our minds to go beyond all of this conditioning to new ways of being.

Examining all of these realms leads us to step two of their program, which they call "Being in the Present—Tracking Your Life Energy" (1992, p. 59). This is a kind of brutal honesty about how many hours you actually put into preparing for and traveling to and from your job, how much spending money is needed to prepare for your job, to heal from job related illnesses, and to reward yourself with expensive purchases for doing the job. With all of the time and money it takes to do our jobs taken into account, the authors propose that you then get to your true hourly wage—about one third of what we are paid per hour. The next part of this step is to track all of your money transactions on paper, as a form of awareness training.

Step three is called "Monthly Tabulation": you study how you are spending your money by categories. This raises awareness even further, preparing us for Step four, "Looking at Three Questions that will Transform Your Life." The first question is, "Did I receive fulfillment, satisfaction and value in proportion to life energy spent? "(1992, p. 113). Question two aims at analyzing our expenditures, asking: "Is this expenditure of life energy in alignment with my values and life purpose." (1992, p. 118).

Finally, question three, "How might this expenditure change if I didn't have to work for a living?" (1992, p.127). The first two questions are self-explanatory. The third asks, if you didn't have to do your forty or more hour a week job, how would your life change, at least in terms of expenditures? Expenditure here refers to the cost of life energy needed. What the authors are getting at here is that first we have to become aware of what traps us on the wheel, and then destroy our illusions about what our real expenditures of life force are, what it costs us, to stay on the wheel. Therefore we can get off the wheel. Once we do this awareness work, we can move towards getting off the wheel of being so attached to ever increasing monetary needs.

One of the keys to this is in knowing when enough is enough; to do this you need accountability to yourself and clear awareness of what the actual flow of money is, which provides an internal yardstick for fulfillment rather than a reliance on externally imposed standards. What you gain from this is a purpose in life beyond acquiring, along with a sense of gratefulness and responsibility, inspiring you to care about your community and the world and live in a way that is sustainable. An additional part of this journey is to that of reconnecting with our spiritual natures. We suddenly have time to meditate, to work on ourselves, to ask ourselves what is the meaning and purpose of our lives and to live closer to this purpose.

Step five is "Making Life Energy Visible."(2002, p. 146) This literally involves making wall-charts, where you graph income and expenses so that you can see your progress. As you move into living with more financial intelligence, you stop buying things and expending energy that you don't really need, allowing you to live out your most strongly held values and your life purpose.

Step six is to minimize spending, and they call this "Valuing Your Life Energy." (1992, p. 170.) This involves consciously lowering our expenses. They give 101 ways to do this, such as living within your means, not going shopping, wear out what you have, take care of what you have, and other such practical steps. They offer advice on how to be smart about credit cards, interest rates, and the like, and then some practical steps for things such as health care, transportation, entertainment, and all other different aspects of daily living.

These authors encourage us to take back our own right to define work without having it strictly tied to paid employment, for instance, doing our life work. Step seven is "Valuing Your Life Energy and Increasing Your Income" (1992, p. 258). Their formula here is "Increase your income by valuing the life energy you invest in your job, exchanging it for the highest pay consistent with your health and integrity." (1992, p. 258).

Step eight is called "Capital and the Crossover Point." This means that each month you total your wall-chart and find out your monthly investment income. The goal is to get to the crossover point where your investment income is higher than monthly expenses, so that eventually you have a source of income separate from your job. The idea is to achieve this point of freedom, so that if we are in a job that does not make sense for us, we are free and safe to stop doing it. It doesn't mean people have to quit work, just that they are free to make changes. We may also be able to work less hours for money without taking a hit financially, giving us more time to volunteer and focus on relationships, spiritual development, and other parts of our lives.

Lastly, step nine is to manage your finances, meaning to know how to make long-term investments and carry out successful asset management. Dominguez and Robin's first choice for long-term investment is in long-term U.S. treasury and U.S. government agency bonds. With this plan, they are talking about one of their main strategies for getting off the wheel is to find a path to early retirement so that you can do the work you love. All nine of these steps of cutting back and focusing your energy are provided with the goals supporting you in making this option available to yourself.

| CHAPTER 8 |

Sage Emery's Abundance Approach

My partner, Sage Emery, has been working with abundance consciousness for many years. She utilizes this approach in working with herself, her clients, and the workshops she teaches. I have witnessed Sage do her abundance work, subsequently filling her therapy practice faster than anyone I have ever seen. Here, in this book is the first time she is sharing her method with the broader public. Her approach is based on the central principle that we are creative beings, connected to everything that exists, and are therefore we are creating all the time, whether we are conscious of it or not. The more conscious and focused we are in our attempts to create, the more effective and efficient our creative efforts become.

This section below is written by Sage Emery:

All of our manifestations are a result of attracting electrons. Electrons represent the energy from the body of God. Electrons are pure universal light substance. They have consciousness. They work at the service of the Divine and their energy is neutral. However, all electrons come from Source energy as "Love." Electrons are created as energy particles from the non-manifest realms waiting to be called into service. Electrons want to respond to Love. We do create at all times with our thoughts, emotions, and actions. We also create from the unconscious parts of ourselves. The electrons will also manifest into reality from our darker parts of ourselves. Electrons serve Life unconditionally, weather created out of Love or negativity.

Our bodies and our energy is designed to create, and we embody the dance between the universal masculine and feminine principles. In this approach, the Sacred Feminine is the un-manifested potential of the universe that hasn't yet taken form, and yet is available and waiting to serve, waiting for the invitation of the Masculine. This is similar to what the Kabbalistic rabbi said in the chapter on Kaballah. The Sacred Masculine energy is manifestation itself. Manifestation is the love affair between these two principles. The Masculine has to put out his desire to know the Sacred Feminine so She comes from potentiality into form.

What follows is her main teaching story around how this works: Once upon a time there was a king. This was a very benevolent king who through his wisdom, power, and love serves the life of his kingdom so that all of the people in his domain are happy and living in a life that is prosperous. The King, through his wisdom looks out at his kingdom and sees a world that is a perfect reflection of himself and is in perfect harmony with who he is at the time of his reign. Something inside of him longs for something new and even a more accurate reflection of himself. The King decides he wants to have a fountain in the middle of his village.

The King lives his life with the understanding that his world is a reflection of who he is internally. He has a profound love affair with the Divine Mother, or Sacred Feminine. In order to have a relationship with her he must enter her realm. The realm of the Sacred Feminine is the un-manifest, where all potential exists. He also understands that he lives in the realm of the Sacred Masculine, which is the realm of our material world of form. He loves the Goddess with all his heart, all his mind—with his entire being. He knows that in order to have a relationship with her all he needs to do is ask and she will provide for him as evidence of her everlasting love for him.

The King decides to ask Her for a fountain. A fountain will give the citizens a place to gather to socialize and collect water. He would like the fountain to be beautiful and a tribute to the Sacred Feminine. Remembering that he is a King, and as a King, he is "entitled" to have what ever he wants, whenever he wants it. He has a solid belief that his subjects will benefit from this fountain and it will assist in serving life as he knows it.

The King brings all his feelings of Love to the Goddess. He pours out love through his heart, through his mind and all of his senses. He tells her how much he loves her and expresses a desire to experience her in relationship. He would like her to express her love of him by creating a beautiful fountain in the middle of the city for him. He will dedicate it to her so that all will know of the love he has for her.

The King enters the realm of the un-manifest of the Sacred Feminine. This is the place where no form exists, but all potential is just waiting to be called into service. He feels the Goddess hearing the love from the King and he feels her love and passion for him. She also sends such waves of love and passion and gratitude to the king for acknowledging their relationship. The fires of love between them are filling his entire being. The Goddess agrees to his request and is so excited to express her love for him through his desires.

The Goddess calls the electrons into service to create the fountain first in her hidden realms. The King sees what a beautiful fountain she has created for him. Once he has seen all the detail, She sends it through to the sacred realm of the Masculine, the realm of form; this as a gift from the Sacred Feminine to her beloved. The King knows that the fountain will come. Although he does not know how it will all work out, he is not worried as he surrenders to her Will.

At that time, the architect, all of the masons, the plumbers and all the other workers who build every detail of the fountain come together, so it is a community effort. The abundance, the energy to manifest, flows throughout the kingdom as many people begin to benefit from the kings request. When the fountain is complete, the Sacred Masculine observes gift of the fountain. He is filled with gratitude and love for the Goddess. Through his wisdom he sees this new reflection of himself. All the people of the community see the fountain as a reflection of themselves and their creative potential, and feel gratitude to the Sacred Feminine.

After hearing this story, our work is to find a way to connect with it and use it to create what we want. Sage says for example, in her life, she wanted to create a health and wellness center, a kind of holistic treatment center that brought together psychotherapists, massage therapists, acupuncture practitioners, and others, housed together in a beautiful building. To do this, she has to first see the Sacred Masculine in herself and that she can affirm that she is "entitled" to have her desires manifest.

Many people get triggered with the word entitled. Spirit wants all of us to know that we are Creator Beings. The more you accept yourself as a Creator Being the more you will understand the word entitlement is simply a knowing that the Universe is at your beck and call twenty-four hours a day every day of your life. You can celebrate that fact. Sage believes in herself and her ability to manifest this center, for her own as well as the common good. She first becomes inspired, and then visualizes every detail of what she wants to manifest. Then she feels her relationship with the Sacred Feminine and how much in love she is with her. Sage feels her deep longing to experience her relationship with the Sacred Feminine. She knows the relationship will be met in the manifestation of the wellness center.

She momentarily drops her perception of herself as Sage Emery, and goes into the realm of the Sacred Feminine through meditation and imagining she is in a realm of no form. This is the place where all potential exists, where all the electrons just waiting for a request are floating. Sage brings her awareness to the Goddess of this realm and feels the excitement and love that the Divine has for Sage, and Sage's request.

Sage feels the thrill and ecstasy of the Sacred Feminine's absolute love of Sage. This part is a very important. It is this reciprocal and loving relationship between the Divine and Sage that must be emphasized. Sage takes her time feeling this love until her heart is expanded and bursting with love. In that sacred realm of formlessness, she pulls all of the pieces together of her request. Sage hears the acceptance of the Divine Feminine to give her her desired holistic center. She observes all the electrons coming together to form her center with as many details as possible.

Once the center is created the Sacred Feminine sends it back to the realm of ordinary reality. Sage lets go and trusts in the will of the Divine, while always carrying an expectation of success and gratitude for the success. As the pieces come together she always acknowledges that her success is coming from the love of the Sacred Feminine as an expression of love towards Sage.

Sage then keeps her intention clear and her energy focused so that she stays with this energy every day until her dream comes to fruition. The next step is to believe in herself and the rightness of her inspiration and then to continue to visualize it as if it already exists. She clears any existing belief systems that may block her feelings of entitlement for her success.

She then talks about it and tells everybody about it as if it is already in process, and gets excited about it filling her dream with love. She fills her being with the personal power to manifest her dream, increase her self-esteem, and follow her inspirations, taking them into the world of action. Meditating is not enough. She must over come her doubts and fears by clearing them and then taking action.

The final step is to walk the talk and to go into action by finding the building, hiring the staff, making the business cards, and doing whatever legwork necessary to make it happen. It is similar to an artistic process, where the art yet to be displayed exists within the artist; he gets excited and tells everyone about what he wants to create, only leaving him with the final, but important steps of buying the canvas and painting.

Granted that we are human beings, it is only natural that fears and limitations arise, and they do so for the purpose of being addressed and worked through. For this, Sage recommends doing exercises to help clear the fears and limitations, such as repeating self-affirmations, i.e, "I have a healing center that makes $100,000," or whatever amount needs to be manifested. It is important for the goal to be a stretch, just over the edge and beyond her comfort level.

After saying this slightly uncomfortable goal out loud to herself, she then feels into her body, notices where there is tension, and follows with going into and processing this tension. She feels into it, and finds a story that goes along with the feeling, and then follows her process through the different channels of experience. She works on family and cultural ghosts, just as I showed how to do in the chapter on relationships, as well as all of possible varying belief systems that are in her way. She acknowledges these, sees where they have served her in the past but no longer help her move forward in her life, and in the spirit of forgiveness and love, finally actively lets these go, replacing them with true and positive, supporting beliefs.

EXERCISE: Manifesting Money

Here is an exercise for you to try yourself and experience the enjoyment of manifesting:

1. Remember that you are a creative being who has the capacity and ability to create.

2. State what you desire to manifest with your creativity.

3. Feel your knowingness that have you have the right to create your desires and inspirations, and how your personal world is a reflection of yourself and is in perfect harmony with who you are.

4. Know that you are ready to have a new reflection of yourself that creates a more accurate experience of yourself.

5. Feel your relationship to the sacred realm of creation. Feel how that realm loves you ecstatically and can't wait to be of service to you.

6. Feel your own excitement to give the Sacred Feminine your request so that you can experience Her in what you are creating.

7. Go into deep meditation, drop your personal identity for a minute and let yourself imagine you are in the world of pure potential, creative energy.

8. Feel your love from this world of oneness, of essence and longing to serve your earthly self. When you hear the request (from the beginning of the exercise), you feel your excitement to be able to manifest for your earthly self.

9. While still in the formless spirit realm, start to pull the vision of your creation together and visualize what will be manifested in every detail possible, then watch yourself sending this vision back to the community where you live.

10. Now begin the process of affirming that your vision will come together and will in fact happen. Gently and gradually bring your awareness back to your body, to the here and now. With great excitement and anticipation, tell all your friends, as if you are pregnant and the baby is coming.

11. Stay in that place of knowing and assuming that it is already happening, and feel in your body all the time that you are open to this and it is with you.

12. As the inspirations come through, act, and do the work that you are supposed to do to help it come into manifestation.

13. Notice wherever the tensions in your body, fears, and limitations come up, and work on them. Are they old family belief systems or cultural belief systems? Create a

figure that represents these and interact with this figure until you can let go of the old belief and move on.

Other Approaches to Abundance Work

Motivational speaker Richard Carlson offers us the basic principles underlying most methods of working on our abundance. In many ways they are similar to an updated version of the positive thinking approaches that were so popular back in the 1950's. Carlson's main assertion is that if we learn to relax, and in a casual yet solid manner take the steps we need to be abundant, things will work out for us.

In his book, *Don't Worry, Make Money*, he says of financially successful people, "They don't worry about money! Interestingly enough, the lack of worry preceded the success, and was not a by-product of it. An inner confidence permeated their entire existence." (1997, p.1-2). He goes on to say that, "And the best part of it all was that, in almost all cases, it appears that the non-worriers, the successful people I was studying, truly loved their lives and the way they spend their time."(1997, p. 2).

Further in his book, Carlson ties this concept to abundance work. He says, "Wealth consciousness suggests a complete absence of money worries; an awareness that there is always plenty of money to go around. People who live true abundance never worry about having enough—they know that creating wealth and affluence is a function of their own mind set."(1997, p. 59). On one level, his approach seems overly simplistic.

Yet, in his book on Kabbalah, recall that Rabbi Bonder talks about tapping into this energetic "bank account" that exists for each individual. Rabbi Bonder talked about luck, and so does Dr. Carlson: "Lucky people are constantly putting themselves in the position to be lucky. In other words, they step up to the plate, they participate, they tell others that they are willing to accept help."(1997, p.215). What he is referring to here is that abundance doesn't just come from the universe, that it also involves some form of right action.

Carlson exemplifies, "Creating your own luck is sort of like planting a garden in an ideal environment. You'll be "luckier" with your plants if you provide the best soil, water, sunshine, and growing conditions. If you don't do these things, you might still get lucky and have a bumper crop, but the odds are far less likely." (1997, p. 216). Luck may simply happen, but his book is about increasing the odds of it happening in the realm of money, by moving from a worry-based to an abundant-based state of consciousness. He adds one more magic ingredient to his soup of success: fun."So be successful and create great abundance, but don't forget to have fun!"(1997, p.218)

One final note about Carlson; his theories and work support such aspects of Taoism and Process Work that connect with the concept of flow. He states, "Money is 'circulation'. It needs to flow. When you are frightened, selfish, or when you hoard everything, you literally stop the circulation."(1997, p. 9). Furthermore, Carlson complements Rabbi Bonder's approach regarding giving, pointing out that when we aren't blocked with fear we are giving to others. Similarly, Rabbi Bonder had talked about the power of tzeddakah, of giving to those in need, and how our giving is important to our thriving financially.

Lee Milteer is a top motivational speaker and the author of *Feel and Grow Rich, How to Inspire Yourself to Get Anything You*

Want. Lee's book brings forward many of the specific attitudes and techniques so popular today in the abundance literature. She talks about the power of being able to manifest. She says, "You have within you all the talent and potential to manifest whatever you want. But there is a price tag. You must feel whatever you want inside of yourself, before you can manifest it into reality. You must feel rich to enjoy what blessing you already have to be able to create more. All success must be created internally before it can be created externally." (1993, p. 3). In this paragraph, Lee essentially sums up her view of what needs to be done and gives the methods on how to manifest.

Lee views choice and personal power as key components of your fate. She uses more cognitive-oriented approaches, such as asking the right questions to open up your mind to all the possibilities, and regulating negative self talk which could limit your potential. She creates questions for waking up and going to sleep to help keep us motivated, open and positive, for example, "What do I have to look forward to today, and be grateful for?"

Lee also believes in creating timelines of our lives, as do I, and asking lots of questions at each developmental marker of our lives. She combines this then with taking authority over our thinking in order to stay in positive tracks, and of programming ourselves for success. Lee gives us detailed instructions in affirmations, one of the tools common in most abundance approaches. Some of hers are similar to Sage Emery's. She always creates positive affirmations in the present tense, embraces the new, and thinks and acts as if they are already true. Lee reminds us to put passion behind our affirmations. Therefore, a part of her method would be to write and say positive affirmations about ourselves, and then begin acting as if they are true.

Lee combines these with another tool that is common to most affirmation paths: positive visualizations. Her basic steps include relaxing and getting in a meditative state, and then making clear goals for what you want or want to create in your life. Next you make a picture, and similar to affirmations, you visualize this as if it is already true and happening in the here and now. The next step is to practice, visualizing this as much a possible, at least two times a day for five to ten days for a minimum of 21 days. The final step is to create an external picture; draw or get something from magazines such as quotes, pictures—whatever you can find that is symbolic of where you are going with your life. Look at these several times a day to help reinforce what you are going after.

Lee continues with recommending a good mediation practice to help you center yourself in general, allowing you to being the most effective in your life. Much of the other approaches she takes have more to do with the conscious mind. She aims to help people develop a burning desire to use all of their selves and all of their potential. This means that truly believing in yourself, and being willing to do what it takes to reach your goals in life, both through taking action and learning to follow your intuition with great accuracy.

Similar to many others writing on and working in this field of money and abundance, Lee takes a broad view of what money is. She states, "Wealth is not just money, because creating money alone will not always bring you happiness. Wealth is being at peace with yourself and feeling fulfilled in what you do. It is enjoying and appreciating your life, your family, and your career."(1993, p. 118). Then once you have this broader view, you can utilize your creativity, thinking, planning, imagination, and intuition to go for what you want. She has seven specific strategies to create prosperity. First, she gives us "The Law of Vacuum." She literally means here to clean out your physical property, and give away what you don't need. Strategy two is "Forgive yourselves, and Forgive others," otherwise too much energy is tied up in past relationship scenes.

Strategy three is "Appreciate Yourself," and here she means especially to treat yourself well, to the finer things in life, and do the same for those you love. She says, "You have to feel successful, worthy, and blessed to be able to attract it into your life." (1993, p. 135.) Strategy Four is "Plan for Prosperity," this means think, plan, and take action, for example, listing your goals for each day. Strategy Five is "The Prosperity Law of Goodwill and Love." She suggests that you in order to create the abundance you desire, you have to be able to live well and get along with others, to work well with people. This means carrying this conscious positive attitude beyond yourself and to others you are in relationship with.

Strategy Six is "Self Love." She explains that it is essential for us to feel worthy of being rich, and whatever else we need and want in life. Finally, strategy seven is "Take Action"; after all this work preparing ourselves to be ready and in the right mind to manifest, we have to take action and go after our dreams in a practical way.

Shakti Gawian is a popular author and teacher of spirituality. In her book *Creating True Prosperity*, she goes another level deeper than Milteer or Carlson. Gawain's fundamental point, similar to Sage's perspective, is that we cannot simply do visualization and positive thinking to get the money to flow because we have deep patterns and psychological issues that will block this flow. Prosperity, according to Gawain, "is the experience of having plenty of what we truly need and want in life, material and otherwise."(1997, p.7).

There are three components to being able to achieve prosperity."1. Discover what we truly need and want. 2. Develop the ability to bring these things into our lives. 3. Recognize, appreciate, and enjoy what we have."(1997, p. 8).

What makes this difficult, she asserts, is that we do not know what we truly want because we are conditioned by society to want everything. Additionally, we have numerous psychological blocks that unless addressed, would stop us from bringing this into our lives even if it were possible for us to have what we wanted. Gawian takes the view, like many of the other authors I present in this book, that prosperity is much more than an issue of money.

Gawain helps us to see four different perspectives, or approaches to our relationship to money. The first is materialism: "From the materialistic viewpoint, we believe that the physical, material world is what is real and important, and that our satisfaction and fulfillment comes from what is around us. Our focus is completely external. Money is the key to getting what we want in the physical realm."(1997, p. 13). While we certainly need to pay attention to our material needs, focusing only on this world limits our inner development, as well as our emotional, spiritual, and other various needs.

Next is the transcendent approach. This essentially frees us from focusing on the material world, through the idea of all material to be an illusion, and somehow a lower realm to be risen above. Fulfillment comes from the spiritual realms, not the material. While this helps us become less attached to the material plane, and helps us go more deeply into the realms of spirit and meaningful living, taking this approach to the exclusion of others denies the importance of our daily physical needs and our emotional lives.

The next approach is the New Age approach, which, in its essence, recognizes the connection between our inner psyche and outer manifestation, and that there is an issue of consciousness that connects the two. The idea is that there is infinite abundance for all; if we could only direct our thinking into what is positive, through the use of tools such as affirmations and positive self-talk, we will get there. The limitations here are that this oversimplifies our individual natures. We need to be able to work on our own unique paths and where they guide us around money. In addition, we cannot neglect acknowledging and working on whatever the wounds are that we carry which would keep us from having the energy to manifest and the belief that we deserve what we manifest.

Finally, Gawain gives us her approach, which is based on the idea that money is energy, and that our money situation is a mirror of our consciousness. She sums it up best in this quote: "For a real shift to take place in our lives, we must become aware of our core beliefs and our deep emotions—especially the ones that have been unconscious. We must be willing and able to heal ourselves, not just on the mental level, but on the spiritual, emotional, and physical levels as well."(1997, p.27).

Gawain goes on to say that, "Generally, both our relationship with money and our experience of prosperity will develop as a reflection of our healing and growth on all levels."(1997, p.29) One area that money especially reveals where our consciousness is at is in our ability to relate to money as power. If we are driven to use money to get power, it reveals how insecure we are; reversely, if we avoid the power that money brings, it can wake us up to the fact that we are afraid of power and have work to do there.

Gawain reveals to us that much of our healing path is to integrate different polarities. These include power and vulnerability; active and receptive; giving and receiving; and doing and being. By seeing these as different roles, we can regain our fluid natures. We do this through self-examination, opening up to our whole selves, realizing what roles or parts of ourselves we are identified with, appreciating our main identity, and then integrating some of the disavowed parts of our selves. For example, if I identify as a doer, I can experiment more with non-doing, or simply being; if I see myself as either structured or flowing, regardless of which one I most strongly identify with, I need to integrate the both sides together.

Similar to the work of Process-Oriented Psychology, Gawain also addresses the realm of money-based addictions, such as shopping and gambling addictions. Gawain says of needs and desires, "a need is something essential for our survival and basic satisfaction. We have needs on all levels—physical, mental, emotional, and spiritual. Our true desires are our yearnings for the things we feel will enhance and enrich our lives and our development." (1997, p. 99) Then she sheds light on false desires: those cravings for things that we are sure we need, but in actuality, don't truly benefit our lives."When we pursue a false craving to the point where we become obsessive and out of control, it becomes an addiction. An addiction appears to satisfy some of our needs momentarily, but not for long, because it does not address our real needs. In fact, an addiction causes an increasing amount of damage and destruction to our lives and the lives of those around us." (1997, 100).

Gawain stresses that we must become aware of our addictions and work on them in order to distinguish between our true desires and our false cravings—even if society may be reinforcing our false cravings. These true desires that we have come from our heart and soul, and our work is to find our connection with these true desires, which we can get in touch with through our meditations and by learning to know and trust our intuition.

Gawain has her steps to prosperity, as do other authors. Her first step is having gratitude for what we already have. Her next step is to become aware of our deep feelings and patterns that program and affect our relationship to money, and her third step is to then doing the healing work necessary to move these old core beliefs. This might involve seeking out therapists, teachers, support groups, and other methods. Step four is to follow our own truth, applying our intuition to the actions we take. Step five is to create a vision of what prosperity looks like for us personally. Step six is to set specific goals for obtaining and fulfilling this vision, and step seven is to then bring out our gifts and our creativity, and not only fulfill our personal needs, but share our gifts with the world. If we can follow the details of all of these steps, then we should be on the path to prosperity.

CHAPTER 9

Taoist Approaches to Abundance

Bennett W. Goodspeed, in his book *The Tao Jones Averages*, introduces us to the applications of Taoism to investing. Even though he writes this in the 1980's, his methods and ideas are still relevant. He is reflecting on important ancient truths still applicable to the modern world. Goodspeed's main view is that most investing is organized according to rational analytic methods, yet the swings and realities of the markets are actually best suited for more right brained, intuitive, feeling based methods. These methods are rarely applied; nevertheless, they are the essence of Taoist principles. He presents the Tao as meaning the "Way—the underlying nature of the universe. It is as if there was a central axis around which everything revolves in an interrelated way."(1983, p.16).

Lao Tse, the founder of Taoism, says that one who can follow the way of nature, the flow of the Tao, can positively influence his or her life by learning to be an expert observer and follower of nature. The Taoist learns to observe nature and accept what is. This is called learning to work with the uncarved block that is the pure, unspoiled, natural essence of all things.

These approaches apply well to investing. Goodspread quotes Lao Tse when he says, "The power of intuitive understanding will protect you from harm until the end of your days. The sage is guided by what he feels."(1983, p. 37). Lao Tse joins Process Work and other approaches in appreciating the realm of feeling and intuition, following nature, and in relating to the essence, or the uncarved block.

He further quotes Lao Tse, "Certain ends are best accomplished without the use of conscious means." (1983, p. 66). Goodspread's chief point is that market changes happen so quickly that we cannot simply use analytic methods. He describes this as "trying to understand running water by catching it in a bucket."(1983, p.79). Goodspread explains that, "In investing in the stock market, it is important to discover or see reality before events can be quantified and then easily identified by the analytic horde."(1983, p.87).

Goodspread asserts that by the time the analysts really get behind certain stocks or trends, it is already too late—the trends are already moving. Thus, in order to keep up with the market trends, we need to access and implement our intuitive skills that can go outside of time and space. Goodspread makes the point that changes often come from outside the area of a market that it impacts; "Broad based readings allow one to spot a change in one field that will impact another. Experts, on the other hand, are vulnerable to being surprised by events outside their specialized area."(1983, p. 95).

He continues, "The inferential process is not analytical but one of synthesis. The reader starts with a great deal of information and synthesizes or reduces it by separating wheat from the chaff. By discarding both opinion and what is expected, Lao Tsu's rule of 'adhering to the genuine and discarding the superficial' is observed." (1983, p. 95). Again, what he is referring to is that the investor (the observer) has an open observing mind, therefore she or he doesn't miss anything by becoming too narrow and specialized.

Goodspeed then goes into describing Taoist Investors. He speaks of the bold thinking displayed by Rogers of the Soros Fund, who made investments everyone had thought were ridiculous. However Rogers knew how to look at the moment and then infer the future. In one of the examples given, Rogers recommended for the Soros fund to sell Avon stock when the price was high, as he began to notice that people were shifting to more the natural look. He sold when Avon was at $130 per share, and within a year, it was at $25 a share.

I too had a similar experience. It was when I had a strong intuitive knowing that I should invest in Whole Foods. This was back before I started investing though; I went into some of their stores in Miami Beach when I was attending a seminar, and was shocked as I had never seen such crowds in a natural foods store. I also read about how Whole Foods was rated one of the best places to work by its own employees. By the time I started investing, I did well in Whole Foods, but would have done far better if I could have bought when I first noticed how Whole Foods was taking off and heard that message from my intuition.

Goodspeed later introduces Ry Neuberger, who at the age of 80 was a figure similar to the old Taoists teachers, emphasizing that even in old age, we can have young attitudes. Neuberger states, "I'd stop living if I didn't have the opportunity to learn something every day."(1983, p.109). Goodspeed quotes Don Kurtz who was in charge of common stock management at his company: "'Things turned out well because no one had any preset ideas on how things worked, and thus were not locked into procedures, bias, etc.'"(1983, p.110) Kurtz employed a light management style that Goodspeed says is similar to Lao Tsu's advice, "'Govern a large country as you would cook a small fish—lightly.'"(1983, p.111).

Goodspeed explains that Kurtz, in his attitude that risk and return are inseparable, carries the spirit of Lao Tsu's teachings, that "opposites find their completion only through each other."(1983, p.113.) Goodspeed cites a female investor, Muriel Lucas. He explains that she became famous for her method of asking everyone around her what they were interested in, enjoying, buying, and using. She would then invest in those companies.

This is astonishingly basic, as is the Tao, nonetheless such concepts are often the most difficult to follow for their being so completely basic. This theme arises again and again throughout this book: the tremendous power in seeing what is, and following what is happening. In conjunction with this method comes the importance of using our whole brain. Goodspeed proposes, "If you learn to give each brain equal voting power, you will have a constitutional balance of power as each mode of thinking has the power to temper the other. As the two sides interact in a balanced way, they can then synergistically build upon the value added by the other half's contribution." (1983, p.138).

This is similar to Process Work's view of deep democracy: not only do we work to maintain a democracy in the world, but inside ourselves with our various parts as well. For all intents and purposes, he is an advocate of *Dreaming Money*. He continues to explore the integration with us: "Left brained, logical investors need to observe the law of reverse effort. When a decision seems so perfect that it can't miss, one should take a walk or "sleep on it" in order to give the right brain an opportunity to participate in the decision. Your right brain will work on your investing even when it is out of your left mind. It will, in effect, be working while you sleep."(1983, p. 138). Here is an investor holding an MBA, teaching the same concepts I have throughout this book *Dreaming Money*; it is essential for us to bring into play not only the wisdom we gain from research and advice, but the art and method of listening to our deepest dreaming selves in order to safely and successfully navigate financial waters.

In the spirit of integrating left brain logic with right brain creativity, I would like to briefly share Goodspeed's "Investment Alphabet": A. Be a light sleeper. B. Be your own judge of value. C. Do not be too sure. D. Stay diversified. E. Avoid the recommendations of experts. F. Value the art of selling. G. Be comfortable with risk taking. H. Stick to what you know. I. Use value guidelines. J. Take your losses. K. Don't procrastinate in decision making. L. Don't churn your account. M. Don't fight the tape. N. Don't just hope. O. Avoid inside information. P. When you feel out of synch, don't play. Q. Avoid formula investing. R. Trust your vision. S. Mistakes are OK. T. Be comfortable holding cash. U. Use both brains. V. Bounce your ideas. W. View yourself as a typical consumer. X. Coincidence is more than chance. Y. Avoid the pied piper. Z. Be patient but move decisively. (1983, p.148-153).

I include this alphabet because these are some additional steps he presents that are part of his practical Taoist approach to investing. He ends his book with another key principle, utilized from the teachings of Lao Tse: "Take care of what is difficult while it is easy, and deal with what will become big while it is small."(1983, p.154).

I like Goodspeed's list because he integrates all levels of Process Work in his advice— the consensus reality practical advice, for example, avoid formula investing, and then something more dreamlike in the recommendation to not just hope; and something more at the essence level when he talks about trusting your visions.

In contrast to the more general applications of Taoist theory to the markets, Laurence G. Boldt, in *The Tao of Abundance*, ventures deeper into Taoist theory and its relationship to abundance. He lists the "Five Fingers of the Tao": The Eternal Transcendent Tao, the Mother Tao, The Tao of the Great Mergence, the Tao of the Ten Thousand Things, and the Social Tao, the Way of Humanity. He proceeds to relate each of these worlds to abundance.

The Eternal Transcendent Tao reflects the well-known concept that the Tao cannot be spoken, "It is a transcendent mystery."(1999, p. XVII). Boldt states, "Yet, if we can listen with an empty mind and open heart, we may hear the Word (Spirit, Tao) from which the words have originated. The words are gateways to the Mystery."(1999, p. XVIII). Presented here is the idea of it being our *relationship to the Tao* that determines whether or not we are guided by It. Boldt relates this to abundance in that modern women and men live their lives feeling cut off from the Spirit; "It is the loss of a living spiritual experience in daily life that, more than anything, breeds the alienation and anxiety that plague modern life. Since we have no means of transcending them (nor even the belief that it is possible do to so) we feel pressured by time, restless in space, trapped in ego. Our preoccupation with material possessions and material achievements both reflects and perpetuates our sense of spiritual emptiness."(1999, p.XX).

The Mother Tao is similar to the concept of the Goddess. The author expresses this: "[with the] silent and shapeless 'womb' of Mother Tao, every existing or potentially existing thing or event resides." (1999, p. XX1). From this perspective we grow to accept what is and to see perfection in everything; "In the context of a mutually arising universe, to say that this or that should not be is to say that the entire universe should not exist."(1999, p. XXIII).

Boldt then explains how this relates to our sense of abundance: "For the Taoist, trusting the Tao is not fundamentally different from trusting ourselves and our own deepest nature."(1999, p.XXIV). These basic ideas of Taoism are not only a philosophy, by a way to live daily life. He says, "Thus, in the image of our cosmologies, we in the West struggle to make things happen and to "make our way in the world," while the Taoist takes the wu-wei, the path of effortless action.

In the West, creativity is something we must actively choose. For the Taoist, creativity is an organic process in which we naturally participate, unless we somehow interfere with it."(1999, p. XXV). Finally, from the perspective of Mother Tao, Boldt shares how time is circular, with ends in beginnings, and beginnings in ends. How many of us who are investors think linearly? The markets, we often perceive, as only going up and up, and we forget about the down present along with the up; perhaps we perceive that now they are down, we pull out, and are left realizing we had forgotten the up that still exists.

Next is the Tao of the Great Mergence, the central idea being that separation and duality are an illusion. Next is the Tao of the Ten Thousand Things."Embracing the Tao of the Ten Thousand Things moves us out of an adversarial role with nature, allowing us to tap into the love and spontaneity that is the source of human creativity (1991p.XXXIV).

What follows is the Taoist approach to science and technology. The Taoist scientific method has to do with being empty-minded, and holding a focused detailed observation of the unfolding of nature. Boldt reminds us of the concept of the uncarved block. The wisdom is intuitive, as we learned in the Tao Jones Averages. This Tao of the Ten Thousand Things builds on the uncarved block view of the world. This is a way of seeing beyond the bottom line thinking of traditional economics."The Taoists offer an alternative view of abundance, one that values maintaining human dignity above acquiring social position, and values the free use of time over the acquisition of money in measuring quality of life." (1999, XXVIII). This is an incredible statement of the core values reflected not only in Taoism, but also in much of the Buddhist and Kabalistic theory I have presented. Also, this concept corresponds with Process Work theory, joining in support of the idea that the greatest wealth attainable is to know and be who we are.

Furthermore, as we go further into developing Earth Based Psychology as part of this work Process Work emphasizes more and more non-doing to balance the doing. Not only is this applicable to money, but to everything else in our lives as well. Lastly, the Social Tao refers to the way people act that is accordance with Tao. This also relates to the proper kind of leader and government.

Concern with the social levels in our world comes out of a sense of compassion for all things. True abundance takes into consideration the well-being of all people. This is what we have said in the other approaches as well."The Social Tao respects the dignity and values the natural gift of every individual, and emphasizes social harmony and cooperation (1999, p. XXXVIII) Here is how Boldt describes the basic principle of his book:

The fundamental principle of this book is that the universe is you and is for you. If you put yourself in accord with the way of the universe, it will take care of you abundantly. To experience this abundance, there is nothing you need to do first. It is not necessary for you to earn one more dollar, get a better job, buy a new home or car, or go back to school. All that is required is that you become aware of the inner process through which you create an experience of lack and struggle in your life, and refrain from doing it. Feelings of abundance and gratitude are natural to the human being, they do not need to be added to or put on. We have only to become aware of how we are resisting and inhibiting this natural state (1999, p. 4).

Boldt argues that we need money because it especially supports our freedom, and Taoists value freedom. Money can buy us time. He says money is a rather simple issue—we just need to know what we want, and what it will cost us to get what we need. He says it should not cost us too much to get what we need, by this he is saying that we do not sacrifice our health, integrity, relationships, happiness and other key parts of our lives. In terms of our needs, Boldt urges us to be clear about distinguishing between true needs of our bodies and souls, and the urge we feel in keeping up with financial social pressures.

He continues, telling us that we have to learn to move out of a scarcity model that permeates our consciousness even when there isn't physical scarcity. He shares three steps for us if we find ourselves living in physical scarcity, aimed had helping us move into abundance: The first step is to be aware of inner and outer sources that reinforce a scarcity model. For example, lets say someone comes from a family where the parents were always talking about their bad luck and that while others could easily be successful, like their friends, they were somehow full of this bad luck. If a child growing up in this system internalizes this, it may become a background program determining to a large degree the financial life of this person.

The second is to grow a spirit of abundance in our lives, appreciating and celebrating what we have, and feeling our connection to all things and to following the Tao. Finally, in his third step we are to become a force of liberation through our interactions with others, helping them to see that we all live in a world of abundance, and how to follow that abundance.

This is similar to concepts of Process Work and rank awareness. If we are aware of our rank, we don't try to hide or deny our abundance but to use the power and freedom this abundance gives us to help others achieve their own abundance. Boldt explains that if the natural state is abundance, we need to develop our receptivity to bring in this abundance.

Taoism values this feminine, receptive approach to life."The Taoist relies principally on the feminine intelligences: intuition, acceptance, and the wisdom of the body." (1999, p.56). This leads us to seeing life in a unified way."The classical Taoists did not see a dichotomy or inherent conflict between spirit and nature. On the contrary, they viewed the spiritual life as the full flowering of the human nature."(1999, p. 69). The author talks of how to break our conditioning toward scarcity, and the association of money with hard work, pain, and suffering: "Abundant living has an easy and effortless quality to it.

If you recognize yourself as being at one with the process that is the universe, if you have opted to receive the bounteous fits of life and of your own nature, you are free to act with ease in a world you feel at home in."(1999, p.85). We move within our world with a sense of oneness with all beings and all of forms of life in nature.

The Taoists believe that in this relaxed state of oneness, our chi, that is, our life energy, can flow."The free flow of 'life energy'(chi) brings spiritual, emotional, physical, even financial health."(1999, p.105.). From this view, Boldt asserts that some experiences of poverty can be explained as the blockage of chi, where our energy is not flowing freely. Not only can we get blocked circulation in our arteries, but in our money flow as well. All of these principles make up the different basic principles of Tao; we have covered the unity of the Tao; the nature of abundance; the ease of abundance, and now the flow of abundance.

What comes next is the power of abundance. Rather than being dominated by social pressures, this concept expresses how we hold true to our innate powers to flow and create. Our true dignity is found in our following our own natures and utilizing the gifts each of us is given. One of the traps that lures us away from following our true natures can be our over-reliance on security.

One purpose of society is to create an atmosphere in which creativity and natural abilities can come forward and flow. Following nature forwards the flow, and following what is unnatural and artificial inhibits the flow. Much of human poverty and inequality is birthed from this opposition to nature. Want to be more successful? Align yourselves with studying and following nature—both your own internal nature and the bigger Nature, the way of the Tao.

The next principle is the harmony of abundance. This is the fundamental concept that yin and yang together make up the whole; the lack of polarization allows us to live in the world in a state of peace and being at home. When we lose this awareness, our thinking naturally shifts into that of wining over another, succeeding at the expense of the other. We move into hostile competition with one another and abandon the spirit of cooperation.

The principle that follows is called the leisure of abundance. It is based on "human–heartedness," that is, compassion for our authentic being. Without leisure, the author explains, we cannot express and relate to others from the very natural place of human-heartedness. For Boldt the main ingredient distinguishing something as leisure is timelessness."To forget time is to forget ourselves, to lose self-consciousness. This loss of self-consciousness is simultaneously relaxing and invigorating. It is the essence of leisure."(1999, p. 202).

The beauty of abundance says that people who are true to themselves and follow their deepest sense of self are not only in harmony with nature, but they reflect and carry a quality of beauty. As the author states, "If we are mainly units of production and consumption, then beauty has not intrinsic value. It is only a commodity like any other, to be sold at a price the market will bear. If, on the other hand, we are spiritual beings, beauty is fundamental to our existence.

Beauty is nourishment for our souls—as necessary to our spiritual growth and well-being as food is to our physical sustenance. Surely, an abundant life is one rich in inner and outer beauty." (1999, p. 262). Beauty is connected to excellence as well."Can we respond to the spontaneous impulse of intuition and yet maintain the persistent effort necessary to achieve excellence?

Chapter 3 examined the principle of wu-wei, or effortless action. Effortless action must never be confused with slipshod work or with a careless or indifferent attitude toward what we are doing." (1999, p. 261). I also appreciate the Taoist attitude that life is a gift. Life has its own wisdom, and the work, as we also say in Process work, is to learn to stay connected to this larger Self, to this way of beauty.

| CHAPTER 10 |

From Heaven to Earth— A 2000's Approach to Self Sufficiency

When I was in my early twenties, I read about a Gestalt Institute in Canada and gained great interest. I have since written extensively about my experiences living in Gestalt Community. In my first book, *Changing Ourselves, Changing the World*, I wrote in great depth about my experiences in this community, a community not only dedicated to the Gestalt approach to our emotions, but to a style of daily living. This style included a Zen-like devotion to awareness and paying attention to details, a heavy does of confrontation, and a particular emphasis on self-sufficiency.

I went from being a fairly pampered young man who didn't know how to cook, check the oil in a car, garden or fix relatively anything, to someone who could cook from several ethnic traditions, bake bread, put in a new carburetor in his Volkswagen, raise hundreds of pounds of food, and take care of some rough billy goats. However, this experience took us far beyond achieving personal self-sufficiency. As a group, we were minimizing our reliance on the outside world. We grew as much food as possible, fixed everything we could, lived on an island with little contact with the mainland, and fixed our own minor health and veterinary crises. This was seen as our way off of the wheel of a modern society that was disconnected from nature, a society that was so expensive to live in, that only by working around the clock could a person hope to survive economically.

Presently, thirty years later, I find that some aspects of this approach are still with me. I continue to live in the country, and do put up food for the winter, but not as much as I used to. I fix more things than I ever thought I would myself. I rely a great deal on my own knowledge of natural healing and mind-body medicine to deal with most of my body symptoms. If I can't deal with it, I go to licensed naturopathic physician who helps me.

All the while, I am a modern person. For my career, I drive a great deal, and fly from city to city and country to country. I have more varying types of insurance than I ever thought I would have, including medical, dental, long–term care, and mortgage disability. My garden production is down, and I don't have time to even change my own oil, more or less repair my car myself. Yet, deep down I know that I could be far more self-sufficient if need be.

During times of possible threat to our relationship, family, community, nation and even global well-being, this knowing is an extremely valuable gift and tool; for example, during such events as the turning of the millennium, when outrageous fear generated around modern systems breaking down, this inner awareness gained from previously mentioned experiences and teachings gave me a deep sense of security.

Another essential part of being self-sufficient is to acknowledge the importance of connecting with the longing for community and connection—something that goes beyond the individual's survival based needs. Self-sufficiency at its essence level might mean having more access to my own being and ability to be centered; from this place, I can reach out to others more, as well as bring more love, connection and healing into the world. I never will forget one of my spiritual teachers who said he always got up very early in the morning so he could really take care of himself. In this way he was self –sufficient, giving himself what he needed first, which allowed him to spend the rest of the day serving others as a powerful healer and guide.

In the old Gestalt based approach of self-sufficiency I have been examining, the emphasis is on materialistic elements, such as growing food and fixing a car. However, being off the wheel of the illusions in the money world not only coincides with skills in the physical world, but these activities also help develop our awareness, just like working on our dreams develops our awareness. To rely on our physical survival skills alongside our awareness will not only help us to survive, but thrive in this world and utilize our success for the benefit of all.

| CHAPTER 11 |

Conclusion

We have examined how money is a solid material matter and also a dreaming process. Our journey into this dreaming process centered on Process-oriented Psychology but also took us into many different ancient spiritual traditions and more modern New Age and alternative approaches. We have discovered that getting free of the system is much more complex than just becoming materially self-sufficient. To begin, there are parts of the system that serve me well, such as health insurance.

In Process work we would say the system is a secondary process, a part of us that also needs to be integrated. For example, much of the structured nature of the system is necessary for individuals and communities needing to become independent of the culture. For example, if you are against how structured the system you work for is, but then can structure more your own life you might be able to start your own business, doing things the way you like them done. Without integrating the system, it will show up unconsciously as oppressive patterns instead of becoming one of our tools to create our own desired lives.

My model of liberation is not only freeing oneself from the material. In the story of Siddhartha, of Buddha becoming Buddha, he first becomes wealthy. In Zen, it is said that it is easier to become detached if you first have. This makes sense to me, and I am no longer against the concept that having is a stage of learning how to be detached and let go.

In fact, as we read in the chapter on Buddhism, poverty isn't a requirement of enlightenment. You can be detached and rich or detached and poor; you can also be attached and rich and attached and poor. The essential teaching here is to develop awareness and learn lessons around money, and to move beyond the illusions that feed the addictions to money.

The more one works on him or herself, the more money becomes a simple tool, a means of achieving one's own rich life goals; accumulation of capital is no longer an end in itself. We learn to become lucid dreamers when it comes to money. We can use our awareness to learn about ourselves, and in our lucid dreaming, can receive guidance from our deepest Selves—our Process Mind Wisdom—to know how to proceed with our investments and other money matters.

We can then learn how to turn this guidance into manifestation, with methods Sage Emery and others teach us. The final stage of dreamwork, whether from a Jungian or Process Work perspective, is to put to use what you have learned about yourself. You must take some action based upon your new insights. Mastering money may also then require very specific knowledge and skills in business, real estate, investments, and other areas of the money world. Without going deeply into these more consensus reality skills of investing, handling money, creating businesses, all the inner guidance and manifesting you do may not produce the results you desire. However, going into the consensus reality tools of generating and money are not the focus of this book.

Our work in this book is to become clear about our path in life, what Mindell calls "A path of heart," and move forward toward this path. These days I think of a path of heart as something that at any moment, if it is my last moment, I can be proud and satisfied that I was walking this particular path in my work, spiritual, financial, relationship, and other parts of my life. A path of heart includes money but doesn't stop there, and is connected with the person feeling that their life has meaning. Following a path of heart means that your daily living is connected to your deepest dreaming.

Remember when we walked the lines of the vectors, as developed by Drs. Amy and Arny Mindell. The central line of the vector is what we are connected to when on our path of heart. This is an unstoppable path. No lack of money or health or anything material can stop us. Even if we are in a coma, we can dream about our path, and take steps in our dreams.

When I ask Mindell about doing this or that, he says over and over to remember to follow that deepest mind, the Process Mind. Money is only meaningful in the context of a life that is meaningful, a life of not only taking care of ourselves and those we love but also reaching out to the planet and using our resources wisely for all beings. That is the mind that has the bigger perspective than that of only myself, this relationship, or this time and this space.

When it is time to focus on making money, we do it, but with the awareness that we do this for some larger purpose; that larger purpose will guide us if we can listen to our dreams and dreamlike experiences. We utilize our financial power not only for ourselves, but to stand for issues of local, national, and global justice, to not only make our lives more rich, but everyone else's as well. Many of the Buddhist teachers have said that true enlightenment can't exist until all beings are enlightened—we can make progress towards enlightenment as individuals, but this is only one step.

The world would be a different place if we also realized that no one person could be truly wealthy as long as much of the world lives in poverty. Money is powerful and can possess us; we must wrestle with it and dance with it and find our own unique way of relating to it. Once we do this work on ourselves and walk the many vectors of our lives, we realize that money is only one source of wealth among many.

We can utilize what Taoism, Buddhism, Kaballah, Process-oriented Psychology, and many of the other great world teachings have to give us in terms of living a life that takes money beyond the material to a spiritual level in our lives. Nevertheless, the greatest teachers of this path are still our own dreams and inner wisdom that keep calling us to be and live with more awareness.

Hopefully this book will contribute to you walking your path of money full of love for yourself and for others. Remember also that Sage's exercises also were about love manifesting itself through the creation of money and other material goods. When I started writing this book, I never thought it would end in talking about love, but here we are, finding that money can and needs to be in the service of love, creating community, nurturing ourselves, and spreading that love around the planet.

Just as the Taoists, we can move into our world of abundance as a path of beauty. This kind of attitude, if held by enough people, would go a long way toward building a world based on peace within ourselves and with our neighbors, along with fostering a world where economic justice is seen as the natural way of life. Of course, in being connected with beauty, we would find ways to make money that simultaneously took care of this beautiful Earth and its ecology. If money and love are fundamentally interrelated and we learn how to best express this oneness, then we would live in a world full of increasing abundance for all, increasing joy and social justice all united together.

BIBLIOGRAPHY

Boldt, Laurence G., *The Tao of Abundance*, New York: Arkana, 1999.

Bonder, Rabbi Nilton, *The Kabbalah of Money*, Boston: Shambala, 2001.

Carlson, Richard, PhD. *Don't Worry, Make Money*, New York: Hyperion, 1997.

Goodspeed, Bennett W. The Tao Jones Average, New York: Penguin Books, 1983.

Gowain, Shakti, *Creating True Prosperity*, Novato, California: New World Library, 1997.

Milliter, Lee, *Feel & Grow Rich, How to Inspire Yourself to Get Anything you Want*, : Norfolk Virginia: Hampton Roads, 1993.

Mindell, Amy. (1995a) *Metaskills: The Spiritual Art of Therapy*. Tempe: New Falcon Publications.

Mindell, Arnold. (1985). *River's Way: The Process Science of the Dreambody*. London: Routledge & Kegan Paul.

Mindell, A. (2007) *Earth-Based Psychology*. Portland: LaoTse Press.

Mindell, A. (2000) *Quantum Mind The Edge Between Physics and Psychology*. Portland: LaoTse Press.

Mindell, A. (1992). *The Leader as Martial Artist*. San Francisco: Harper.

Mindell, A. (1995). *Sitting in the Fire*. Portland, Oregon: Lao Tse Press.

Mindell A.. (1990). *Working on Yourself Alone*. London: Penguin Arkana.

Mindell, A. (1989). *The Year 1*. London: Penguin Arkana.

Mindell, A. (1987). *The Dreambody in Relationships*. London: Routledge & Kegan Paul.

Mindell, A. (1985a). *Working with the Dreaming Body*. London: Routledge & Kegan Paul.

Mindell, A. (1985b). *Rivers Way*. London: Routledge & Kegan Paul.

Mindell, A. (1981). *Dreambody*. Boston: Sigo Press; London: Routledge & Kegan Paul, 1984; Portland, OR: Lao Tse Press, 1998.

Mindell, A. (2002). *The Dreammaker's Apprentice*. Charlottesville, VA: Hampton Roads.

Mindell, A. (2000a). *Dreaming While Awake*, Charlottesville, VA: Hampton Roads.

Mindell, A. (2002) *The Deep Democracy of Open Forums*, Charlottesville, VA: Hampton Roads.

Mindell, A. (2000). *Quantum Mind*. Portland, OR: Lao Tse Press.

Mindell, Arnold and Mindell, Amy. (1992). *Riding the Horse Backwards*. London: Penguin Arkana.

Mindell, A. (2010) *Process Mind*, Wheaton, Ill: Quest Books.

Needleman, Jacob, *Money and the Meaning of Life,* New York: Doubleday, 1991.

INDEX

2000's Approach 197, 199

A

absolute money-maker 128
abundance 11, 22, 24, 39-40, 45, 156, 168, 173-4, 176-7, 183, 185, 187-95, 204, 207
abundance consciousness 155, 159, 165
abundance work 158, 165, 173
actions, effortless 189, 194
addiction 9, 25, 75, 121-3, 127, 151-5, 157, 159, 161, 163, 180, 202
addictive stock market playing 122
addictive tendencies 35, 75, 151
affirmations 175-6, 179
    positive 175
age 21, 69, 85, 87, 160, 185
Aikido 121, 123, 129
Amy 203, 207-8
analytic 89
animals 25, 79, 89, 130
anti-money 13
anxiety 26, 29, 131, 188
Arnold 91, 96, 100, 207-8
associations 35, 79, 89, 192
attachments 37, 129
attitudes 30, 45, 132, 149-50, 175, 186, 195, 204
Atzilut 41
authors 23, 28, 159-63, 174, 178, 181, 188, 192, 194
awake 8, 62-3, 74, 92, 94, 99, 144, 208
awakening 33-5, 88, 99

B

Baal Shem Tov 42-3
background wisdom 54-5
balance 15, 26, 28, 39, 43, 129, 131, 151, 190
battle 145
beggars 16, 87
belief 42, 54, 56, 84, 158, 171, 173, 179, 188
belief systems 66, 143, 170-1
bills 9, 11, 25, 106, 131, 133
block, uncarved 183-4, 190
body sensations 61, 93, 122
Boldt 188-94, 207
Bonder 38, 44, 47, 207
borrow 119, 153
Boston 207
brains 186-7
brakes 113
break money addictions 154
Breaking Money Addictions 154
breathe 97, 99
breaths 106-7
    few 96, 98, 105, 107
Buddha 22-3, 201
Buddhism 8, 22-3, 26, 30, 202, 204
Buddhist Thinking and Money 22
Buddhists 26, 28, 46, 131
businesses 40, 74, 155-6, 201-2

C

calls dreamtime 94
career 57, 67, 121, 148, 157, 176, 198
Carlson 173-4, 177, 207
cast 39, 78-9
center 85, 112-13, 169, 176
    wellness 168-9

channels 9, 42, 61-2, 79, 92, 153, 171
   sensory 61-2, 65
Charlottesville 207-8
chest 93
chop wood 131
circulation 174
cities 57, 73-4, 135, 167, 198
classes 32, 77, 85, 88, 114, 133, 156
   teaching dreamwork 78
clients 8, 12-13, 17, 47, 53, 56-60, 65, 88-90, 93, 109, 116, 121, 142, 152-3, 159
closet 117
clothes 111
   beautiful 117
cloudy 96, 98
college 111-13, 120
combinations 40, 61, 111-12, 135, 139
comfortable 11, 85, 187
community 29, 88, 113, 155, 163, 168, 172, 197-8, 201
companies 111, 185-6
companions 35
compassion 73, 147-8, 190, 194
conflict 53, 55, 59, 85, 141, 143, 146, 192
connect 40, 43, 77, 108, 122, 129, 168, 174
connection 9, 14, 24, 41, 55-6, 58, 87, 122-3, 132, 179, 181, 192, 198-9
consciousness 11, 25, 32, 34, 40, 49, 58, 64, 78, 155-6, 165, 174, 179, 191
consensus reality 23, 41-3, 62-4, 94, 109, 187
consensus reality skills 8, 202
contact 34, 54, 97
cook 186, 197
cost 43, 45, 162, 191
counseling job 112-13
countries 64, 72, 86, 148, 198
county 116

couples 16, 53, 57, 62, 70, 135-8, 140-3, 145-6
CR 63-4
cravings, false 180-1
creation 48, 171-2, 204
creativity 57, 129, 156, 171, 176, 181, 189, 193
Creator Beings 168
crisis 32, 115-17
crossover point 164
cultural ghosts 145, 148, 171
culture 21, 31, 58, 62, 64, 67, 112, 145, 148, 150, 152, 160-1, 201

D

dad 70, 77, 126-7
daily money decisions 63
dance 60, 80, 95, 107, 166, 204
death 32, 35, 48, 132
debts 136, 139
deepest dreaming nature 8
democracy 186
deposits 45
depth 30, 32, 83, 89, 95, 148
desperation 74, 148
detachment 45, 63, 104, 129, 146, 160
dimensions 34, 46-8, 95
direction 17, 61, 63, 66, 68, 100-2, 104, 144, 151-2, 159
disaster 132-3, 146, 158
disparities 72-3, 140, 155
diver 91
Diversity and Money Arrangements 135
Divine 165, 169
dollars 16, 72, 84, 118, 125, 149, 191
Dominguez 159-60, 164
Dominic 23-4
dream-body concept 57
dream catcher 78
dream classes 88
dream content 93
dream contin 79

dream energy 80
dream figures 79
dream images 58
dream interpretation 80
dream interpreters 78
dream levels 94
dream recall 88
dream relationship 119
dream shifts 81
dream symbols 79, 89, 103
Dream Vector Work 103
dream work 57, 133
dream world 92
Dreamaker's Apprentice 92
Dreambody 92, 207
dreamers 59, 78
  lucid 202
dreaming 16-17, 58, 62-3, 65-6, 77, 80, 88, 92-4, 114, 116, 119, 139, 208
  deepest 203
  hour 42, 95
  lucid 94, 202
  the 58
Dreaming Body 207
Dreaming Money 7-10, 12, 53-4, 184, 186-8, 190, 192, 194, 198, 202, 204, 208
Dreaming-Money-Reiss 109, 138, 147
dreaming nature intact 9
dreaming natures 8-9
  larger 117
dreaming process 15, 17, 71, 109, 117, 128, 201
dreaming realms 15, 94, 122
dreaming the dream onward 80
dreaming worlds 47, 109, 158
dreamland 62-3, 94
dreamland guides 63
dreamlike 8-9, 44, 188
dreamlike experiences 16, 42, 203
  daytime 87
dreamlike phenomena 43
Dreammaker 76

Dreammaker's Apprentice 207
dreams 8-9, 13-16, 57-8, 75-84, 86-94, 101, 103-4, 109-10, 116-17, 119, 121-3, 125-8, 139-40, 158, 203-4
  access 92
  collective 64
  dictive 77
  high 138-40
  realms of 43, 47
  remembering 88
dreamt 12, 14, 77, 82, 88, 93
dreamtime 62, 94
dreamwork 14, 79, 88, 114, 202
dreamwork methods 63
dreamy, very 157
drinking 67

E

Earth 18, 100, 102, 104-7, 130, 144, 157, 197, 199
Earth spot 105-7
economic disparity 73, 137
economic rank 74, 86, 147
economics 73-4, 85
edge figures 66-7, 95
edges 64, 66-8, 80-1, 83, 93-5, 170, 207
electrons 165-6, 168-9
emotional 38, 161, 178-80, 193
emotions 61-2, 93, 160, 166, 179, 197
energy 13, 23, 45, 48, 54, 59, 76, 79-80, 83, 91-2, 95, 105-7, 164-6, 170, 179
  potential 41, 48, 66, 128
engine 114, 133
enlightenment 34, 94, 118, 130-1, 133, 202, 204
Eternal Transcendent Tao 188
ethical 119
Eugene 114-15, 135, 142
excellence 194
excitement 141, 169, 172
Exodus Rabbah 39

expenditures 29, 162
expenses 12, 27, 163, 194
experiential 89

F

facilitator 53-4, 60, 65
Family Issues and Money 135, 137, 139, 141, 143, 145, 147, 149
family money issues 144
family money playing video poker 152
father 11-14, 77, 110-11, 114, 116, 122, 126, 131, 148
fears 27, 32, 34, 131, 146, 170, 172, 174
FI thinking 160
fights 120, 124, 142-3, 148, 153, 187
finances 15, 17, 68, 75, 133, 136-7, 139, 142, 164
financial 7, 16, 28, 41-2, 140, 203
financial dream advisor 18
financial goals 104
financial integrity 160
financial relationship 142, 144-5
  non-traditional 137
financial worlds 18, 55-6
Finding Freedom 155, 157, 159, 161, 163
flickers 95, 100
flirts 47, 95-6, 98
Flirts to Money Issues 98
food 39, 58, 112, 133, 147, 194, 197-8
Foods 120, 185
Forgive 177
formula 163, 187-8
fountain 166-8
  beautiful 167-8
Fred 138
free will 40
freedom 9, 63, 89, 108, 112, 147, 164, 191-2
frenzy, feeding 156
fueling 122-3, 152
fulfillment 161-3, 178

funeral 35

G

gambling 91, 151-2
Gates family 73
Gawain 177-81
gender 85
Gestalt therapy 113-14
gifts 30, 47, 110, 158-9, 168, 181, 193, 195, 198
global money set 11
God 34, 131, 165
Goddess 167-9, 188
gods 27
Goodspeed 183, 185-7, 207
Goodspread 184
Google 120-1, 123-6
  next morning 124-5
grandparents 110, 112
grant 12, 116
gratitude 167-9, 181, 191
Great Mergence 188-9
ground 124, 157
groups 60, 63-4, 70, 87, 156, 197
guidance 16-17, 76, 104, 202
guide 9, 54, 63, 75, 87, 179, 199, 203

H

haggard 151-2
Hampton Roads 207-8
harbor 82-3
harmony 21, 159, 193-4
Hating Money 111
health 32, 43, 85, 121, 123, 126, 151, 164, 168, 191, 203
heart 33, 38, 48, 167, 169, 181
  path of 203
heaven 39-40, 130, 197, 199
hell worlds 26
helping 14, 72, 84, 107, 146, 191-2
hierarchies 27, 84-5
hindrance 32
home 109, 124, 132, 191-2, 194
home repair 132

horse 89, 91, 161
hour lucid dreaming 94
house 12, 35, 81-3, 116, 124, 126, 132, 158-9
human-heartedness 194
human life 32-3
human world 28
hungry ghosts 25-6
hurt 109, 139-40

I

identification 64
illusions 23-4, 31, 33, 127, 159, 162, 178, 189, 199, 202
imagination 58, 90, 101, 106-7, 154, 176
imagining 90, 169
income 10, 116, 148, 151, 163-4
incompleteness 24
independence 138
India 16, 86
indigestion 58
infinite 41
inflame 85
inner scan 97, 99
inspirations 170-2
intention 127, 148, 158
intentional awareness 78
intuition 42, 119, 176, 181, 184-5, 192, 194
investments 11, 14-15, 17, 46, 48, 77, 118, 120, 124, 131, 160, 185, 202
    long-term 164
investors 184, 187, 189
island 112, 197
issues 15, 18, 24, 41-2, 54-5, 63, 73-5, 84-6, 96, 98, 135-8, 142-3, 150, 156, 203

J

Jane 138-9
jealous-gods 27
Jeff 148-9
Jews 37-9

Jim 137
journey 12, 15, 31, 38, 122, 131-2, 163, 201
jump 139
Jungians 80, 90, 202
justice 39, 44, 71

K

Kabbalah and Money 37, 39, 41, 43, 45, 47, 49
Kabbalah of Money 37, 62, 207
Kathy 146-7
Katrina 124-5
Kegan Paul 207
king 166-7
King 166-8
kingdom 166, 168
knowing 25, 44-5, 54, 66, 78, 82-3, 125, 149, 162, 168, 172, 198
knowledge 32, 46, 71, 198, 202
Kulanada 23-4
Kurtz 186

L

Lao Tse 21, 44, 129, 183-4, 187
Lao Tse Press 207-8
Lao Tsu 184, 186
LaoTse Press 207
lawyer 113
learning 12, 44-5, 48-9, 70, 96, 99, 111, 119-20, 131-2, 147, 157, 160, 176, 181, 183
Lee 175-6, 207
leisure 28, 194
lessons 45, 83, 127, 202
life energy 161-4, 193
lifetimes 41
Liking Money 110
limitations 81, 93, 170, 172, 179
lines 30, 35, 46, 58, 63, 69, 101-4, 106, 118, 144-5, 159, 203
literal 78-9
literal level 76, 78

live 8, 22, 24, 27, 72-3, 112, 114, 140, 146-7, 149-50, 163, 172-3, 192-3, 198, 204-5
livelihood 40, 45-6
long-term homosexual relationship 141
losing 15, 56-7, 82, 110, 118, 120-1, 127-8, 153
losses 21, 54-6, 82-3, 127-9, 187-8, 194
lottery 65, 90-1
love affair 166
luck 40, 42, 46, 48, 174
  bad 191-2
lucky 174

M

magic 158-9
Make Money 173, 207
manifest 38, 159, 166, 168-72, 175, 177, 179
manifestation 58, 165-6, 169, 172, 179, 202
Manifesting Money 171
marginalize 44, 78, 80, 152
markets 14, 38, 44-5, 57, 77-8, 81-4, 109-10, 118-19, 121, 123, 125-9, 131, 183-4, 188-9, 194
marriage 32, 114-16, 152, 157
marry 133, 136
Masculine 166, 168
Mastering money 202
material wealth 48-9, 147
materialism 21, 33, 111, 160, 178
mazel 46
media 7-8
meditations 33, 53, 114, 169, 172, 181
merit 41, 48
midst 8, 15, 116, 118, 130, 153, 158
Mindell 42, 57-60, 62-4, 92, 94, 105, 203, 207-8
Mindell, Arnold 12, 17, 53, 55, 61, 79, 83, 105, 116, 125

Mindell calls 24-hour dreaming 100
miracle 13, 82-3, 117
model 39, 142-3, 201
money 7-19, 21-4, 29-34, 37-9, 43-9, 65-73, 86-8, 98-104, 106-11, 113-25, 127-33, 135-49, 157-64, 176-9, 201-5
  associated 128
  confused 30
  connect 128
  creating 176
  first decent 66
  handling 202
  hoarding 151
  investing 54
  investment 120
  less 68, 139
  liked 110
  linking 31
  losing 151
  making 7, 15, 33, 46, 56, 68, 84, 86, 120-1, 128-9, 151, 203
  managing 8
  manifest 8, 128
  most 111
  navigate 63
  our 139
  ourselves surrounding 65
  power 31
  rooted beliefs surrounding 149
  sized 57
  spending 151
  value 129
money addictions 25, 35, 159
money arena 33, 37
money arrangements 135, 142
money-based addictions 180
money behavior 28
money consciousness 10
money difficulties 9
money dreams 13, 77, 87-8
money effects 62
money factor 32
money flows 54, 193

Money Guidance 108
money helping mom 70
money issues 17, 30, 55, 70, 75-6, 96, 98, 101, 105-6, 108, 138, 142, 160
money lenders 37
money life 42, 62
money markets 45
money mess 81
money moments 102
    most ecstatic 102
Money Path 101, 204
Money Problems 98, 106
money realms 38, 56
money relationship 139
money situations 43, 130, 179
money transactions 162
money work 96
money world 71, 103, 111, 199, 202
money worries 173
Most dreams 78
mother 111, 148
Mother Tao 188-9
mountain 105, 131-2
movement 34, 60-2, 80, 92-3, 95, 97, 99-100, 105-8, 144, 154
movement signal 154
mystics 42

N

natural 115, 139, 160, 170, 185, 191
natural state 161, 191-2
nature's path 54, 56
navigate 17, 56, 65, 71
navigating 17, 65
Needleman 30-5, 208

O

objects 24, 63, 94
oil 133, 197-8
oneness 95, 107, 130, 172, 193, 205
Oregon 114-15, 130, 135, 157, 207
Oregon Coast 81, 124, 158-9

P

pain 28, 39, 60, 128, 192
paint 78, 80
parallel worlds 47-8
parents 11, 66, 110, 112-13, 191
partner 102, 118, 124, 137-41, 143, 145-7, 149, 165
passion 67, 167, 175
path 9, 14-15, 17, 22, 35, 44, 58, 63, 68, 70, 84, 110, 114, 127, 202-4
Paul 141, 152
peace 55-6, 74, 83-5, 112, 126, 176, 194, 204
Penguin Arkana 207-8
penny stock market 118
people dream right 93
person 11, 17, 39, 41, 72, 74, 77, 79-80, 85, 91-3, 135, 146, 152, 160, 192
personal 14, 64, 75, 105, 181
personal power 170, 175
perspective 41, 54, 84, 95-6, 98, 104, 143, 145-6, 161, 178, 189
physical 161, 178, 180, 193
physical scarcity 191
picture 79, 93, 96, 98, 176
    momentary 97-8
planet 10, 39, 104, 160-1, 203-4
pocket 12, 38
polarities 17, 63, 104, 107, 146, 149, 180
pops 79, 89
Portland 207-8
Positive addictions 152
positive karma 41
poverty 27, 39, 43, 45, 54, 72, 86-7, 118, 151, 155, 193, 202, 204
poverty-consciousness 155
power 23, 27, 31, 34, 74, 84-7, 89, 117, 128, 136, 152, 174-5, 179-80, 186, 192-3
practitioners 59
prejudices 37-8
preparing 49, 161-2

price 25-6, 31, 185, 194
Primary and Secondary Processes and Money 69
private practice 12, 93, 157
Process Mind 105, 107, 131, 203, 208
Process-Oriented Aproach 110, 114, 116, 118, 184, 186, 188, 190, 192, 194, 198, 202, 204, 208
Process-Oriented Psychology 8, 12, 16, 23, 31, 40, 42, 45, 47, 53, 88-9, 91, 100, 129, 140
Process-Oriented Psychology and Dreaming Money 55, 57, 59, 61, 63, 65, 67, 69, 71, 73, 75, 77, 79, 81, 83
Process Work 16-18, 23, 47, 53-5, 57-62, 70-1, 73-5, 83-4, 92-3, 95-6, 104, 121-2, 151-2, 186-7, 201-2
Process Worker 42, 55-6, 58-9, 72
projects 37-8, 115
prosperity 176-9, 181
protests 111
psychology 12-13, 15-16, 105, 139, 207
Psychology and Dreaming Money 53

Q
Quantum Mind 207-8
quit 26, 66-7, 82

R
Rabbi Bonder 38-9, 41, 43-9, 62, 86, 128, 173-4
rabbis 39-40, 46-8
races 85, 120
rank 23, 28, 73-4, 84-7, 136, 143, 192
reality 9, 24, 32, 37-8, 43, 62-4, 72, 76, 88, 139-40, 159, 166, 175, 183-4
    everyday 8, 58, 63, 87
recommendations 66, 119, 187-8
refrigerator 76

Reiss, Gary 109-10, 114, 116, 118, 138, 147, 184, 186, 188, 190, 192, 194, 198, 202, 204
relationship 9, 37-8, 62, 77, 95, 101-3, 106-7, 115, 118, 121-3, 129-30, 137-49, 166-7, 169, 177-9
    co-parenting 115
    creative 24
    everyday 109
    fantastic 126
    father's 149
    individual 17
    long-term 77
    loving 169
    plague 138
    positive 16
    working 115
Relationship Body 140
relationship channel 62
relationship crisis 84
Relationship Dreambody 140
relationship dynamic 143
relationship issues 93, 145
relationship partner 142, 144
relationship problems 56, 70, 75, 140, 148
relationship process 24, 80
relationship role-playing 80
relationship scenes 177
Relationship Vectors and Money 102
relaxation 128-9, 143
religions 33
repairs 11, 132-3
request 167, 169, 172
resources 18, 135-6, 203
riches 22, 45, 47
ride 89, 114, 133
right brain 187
risk 83, 91, 186-7
river 96, 98, 105, 124
River's Way 58, 60-1, 207
Rogers 185
Routledge 207
Routledge & Kegan Paul 207

Rumi 35

S

Sacred Feminine 166-70, 172
Sacred Masculine 166-8
safe harbor 82, 84, 125
safeguard 48
safety 32, 83, 125, 138
Sage 157-8, 168-70
Sage Emery 165, 169, 175
Sage Emery's Abundance
  Approach 167, 169, 171, 173,
  175, 177, 179, 181
Sam 65, 136
Sandy 146-7
savings 12, 26, 28, 146, 160
scan 105, 107
scarcity model 156, 191
seals 79
secret 22
Seguallah 41
segulah 40
self 8, 16, 21, 23-4, 34, 69, 97-8,
  176, 180, 194, 199
  deepest 9, 17, 105, 107, 122, 202
  deepest dreaming 187
  earthly 172
self-consciousness 194
self-destructive patterns 139
self-sufficiency 197, 199
Self Sufficiency 197, 199
sensations 62-3, 94
sentience 63, 76, 95
sentient 63, 94-5, 97, 141
sentient level 62, 75-6, 97
sentient realms 95-6
separateness 23, 139-40
separation 7, 137-8, 189
service 12, 33, 46, 165, 167-8, 171,
  204
Shelia 136
ship 82-3, 91
  big 82
  little 82-3, 125
shopping 153, 161, 163, 180

signals 60-1, 65, 77, 154
  double 69
skills 60, 117, 148, 199, 202
small amounts 119
smell 61-2, 106-7
social issues 10, 17, 62, 70-1, 86
Social Issues and Process Work 70
social rank 24, 85
Social Tao 188, 190
society 8, 37, 43, 71, 85, 178, 180,
  193, 198
Soros Fund 185
souls 39-41, 45, 181, 191, 194
space 34, 63, 69, 77-8, 129, 138,
  140, 184, 188, 203
spiritual 7-8, 11, 32, 66, 118, 132,
  178-80, 193, 203
spiritual channels 62
spiritual life 7, 13, 16, 23, 192
spiritual path, authentic 34-5
spiritual rank 85, 87
Spiritual Traditions and Money 19
spirituality 7, 12-13, 15, 17, 87, 114,
  118, 129, 132, 177
spot 97, 99-100, 105-7, 184
squirming 69
St. Louis 110, 114
stock market 11, 14-15, 35, 42-3,
  54, 57, 65-6, 77-8, 109, 111, 117-
  19, 127, 129, 131, 133
stock market adventures 124
stock market experience 123
stock market torture 124
stocks 77, 82-4, 114, 118-20, 124-5,
  184
stories 17, 39, 41, 47, 53, 80, 109-
  10, 123, 158, 168, 171, 201
Story 51, 109, 111, 113, 115, 117,
  119, 121, 123, 125, 127, 129, 131,
  133
Strategy 177
strengthen 88-9
stress 58, 81, 111, 128, 146
struggles 18, 97-8, 106, 147, 191
style 40, 132, 197

suffering 16, 39, 73, 85-7, 192
symbols 78-9, 90-2, 103, 124
symptoms 57, 66

T

Take time 70, 102
Tao 21, 56, 183, 186, 188-90, 192-3
Taoism 8, 55, 183, 189-90, 204
Taoist Approches to Abundance 185, 187, 189, 191, 193, 195
Taoist theory 188
Taoists 56, 183, 189-90, 192-3, 204
taste 61, 76
teachings 38-9, 42, 45-6, 83, 87, 93, 96, 187, 198, 202
tension 26, 137, 171-2
terrifying 116, 131
themes 16, 21, 70, 88, 186
therapist 53-4, 56, 58, 60, 65, 93-4, 117, 135, 181
thief 45
time slots 69-70
timeline 69-70, 132
togetherness 138, 140
tools 9, 24, 91, 96, 176, 179, 198, 201-2
town 22, 64, 112, 114
 small 115-16
trauma 142, 148, 150, 155
treasure 40, 47-8
treasure chest 91, 93
trusting 188-9
truth 34, 109, 181
tzedakah 44-5

U

un-manifest 167
unconscious 64-6, 85, 179
 the 58
universe 9, 39, 43, 46, 68, 105, 108, 117, 158-9, 166, 169, 174, 183, 189, 191-2
Universe and Money Guidance 108
unknowing 96, 98

V

vector work 100
vectors 100-3, 141, 144-5, 203-4
vision 32, 60-1, 172, 181, 187-8
visualize 61, 169-70, 172, 176
vitality 9-10
voices 67, 148
 cultural 66-7, 150

W

walking 100-4, 141, 144-5, 157, 203-4
wallet 92
walls 96, 98, 132
water 22, 71, 131, 167, 174
not we 64, 141
wealth 11, 15, 21, 23, 27-8, 39, 41, 43, 45, 47-9, 54, 63, 71, 73, 176
 true 48
wealthy 11, 45, 72, 88, 156, 201, 204
wealthy family 146
wheel 9, 24, 45-6, 129, 153, 159-60, 162, 164, 198-9
wings 22
winners 88
winning 56-7, 65, 91, 121, 127, 153
 agonizing stock market 153
wisdom 9, 14, 17, 21-3, 25, 27, 29, 31, 33, 35, 37, 54-5, 84, 103-5, 166
world project 75
worry 114, 117, 147, 173, 207

Y

your money or your life 35